How schools work

How schools work

Rebecca Barr • Robert Dreeben
with Nonglak Wiratchai

The University of Chicago Press
Chicago and London

The University of Chicago Press, Chicago 60637
The University of Chicago Press, Ltd., London

Library of Congress Cataloging in Publication Data

Barr, Rebecca.
  How schools work.

  Includes bibliographical references and indexes.
  1. School management and organization. 2. Classroom
management. 3. Group work in education. 4. Individual-
ized instruction. I. Dreeben, Robert. II. Wiratchai,
Nonglak. III. Title.
LB2805.B312 1983   371.2   83-6904
ISBN 0-226-03811-4
ISBN 0-226-03812-2 (pbk.)

For Mike and Dan

Contents

Preface

American education is highly individualistic. We find clear expression of this in the importance that parents ascribe to how well their children do in school in the belief that performance there carries weight in determining future life chances—further education, work, career, and earnings. We find other expressions of it in the character of the schools themselves: their emphasis on grading and testing, preoccupation with guidance and social adjustment, and attempts to ascertain that schoolwork has been completed independently. Even the language and rhetoric of teachers extol individual effort—doing well and trying hard; and most particularly, they celebrate the importance of individual differences and the adaptation of teaching to those differences. It is no surprise, then, that with such great stress on individuals—their motivations, goals, mental functioning, and learning—the study of education has been so congenial to the interests of psychologists. A psychological perspective, even among nonpsychologists, has governed the most pervasively asked question about schooling: what are the characteristics and experiences of individuals that influence their learning and achievement?

Some of those experiences, of course, have been tied to the qualities of schools. And while there has been substantial interest shown in the association between school characteristics and learning, comparatively little is known about the nature of the schools themselves and how they work as productive enterprises: what are their parts? how do the parts fit together? how are resources acquired, allocated, and used? and how do schools work as coherent organizations to produce a variety of values? We are interested here in the conditions that influence learning; but we are somewhat more interested in the social organization of schools and how schools work.

As much as this book is about social organization, it is also about teaching. Through the late 1960s and into the 1970s, a conception of teaching emerged as an occupation without a clear technology, one in which it was not possible to identify direct lines of influence between what teachers did in the classroom and the results achieved. More than that, teaching was viewed as lacking a technical language that described and conceptualized the nature of the work. It was portrayed as being shaped more by the vicissitudes of moment to moment events and social interactions than by rational choices and calculations based upon an understanding of cause and effect. Personal style and intuition derived from experience and manifest in ineffable ways were believed to be the hallmarks of the occupation.

We have reason to doubt parts of this conception; for while the language and rhetoric of teaching might indeed be rather spongy, we have found that first grade teachers act in ways that indicate good technological sense. They use grouping arrangements that are well adapted to the social constraints of their classes, alter those arrangements if they become unworkable by moving children along or moving them back according to how well they do, allot time in accordance with the difficulty of the materials they use, and proceed instructionally at rates proportional to the ability levels of the groups they have created. And while we found variations from teacher to teacher in the ways they instruct, their conduct is strongly patterned despite individual differences in style and preference. They manage similar kinds of contingencies in similar ways, and indeed act as if technological principles do underlie their work—uncodified principles to be sure. We would not expect to find such clear patterns of conduct, however, if teachers were in fact guided primarily by personal style and intuition or engrossed in the immediacy of present events.

While this book is not explicitly about school administration, it nevertheless has interesting implications for the work of school principals. Much of the interest in the principalship centers around the theme of leadership and its effect on morale; but good morale does not itself create productivity nor does bad morale necessarily destroy it.

We believe that the principal's influence on learning stems not from leadership in the traditional sense but from inconspicuous events related to the allocation of resources to classes. Among these events, principals, by deciding which children will be in which classroom, establish the distribution of youngsters' social and mental characteristics that in turn sets constraints on the alternatives teachers will face designing workable arrangements for instruction. How a principal assigns the more and less mature children, the bright and the not so bright, the aggressive and the even-tempered is of the essence. The less tractable the class—the more children with low ability, who are immature, and who are disruptive—the fewer viable forms of instructional organization that become available.

In addition to composing classes, principals take responsibility for distributing learning materials and providing modest sums of money to supplement prevailing supplies. They also establish a time schedule that governs which desirable and undesirable places and time periods will be available for the school's instructional and noninstructional activities.

There is a patent irony in how school administration has conventionally been viewed. The influence of principals has been sought in overt forms of leadership and supervision, in kinds of relations presumably tied to their position of authority but whose effects do not readily penetrate the classroom door. Nowhere does this view recognize that the principal's significant influence lies in the allocation and shaping of the school's most basic resources: children's characteristics, learning materials, and time. But these influences are generally established, not in conspicuous social encounters, but in activities usually denigrated as clerical chores in which charts are filled in and names put to paper. These quiet influences, however, shape the conditions under which teachers work; they constrain the forms of instructional organization and influence learning indirectly yet powerfully.

This book, finally, is about first grade reading, and that fact colors what we found and how we think about the effectiveness and organization of schooling. We believe that the prospects for first graders look bright. This is because the great majority of children we studied made considerable progress in an area of the school curriculum which is perhaps the most basic, the one upon which almost all aspects of the later school curriculum depends. Prospects also look bright because the slow reading progress discovered in some of the classrooms could be accounted for by patterns of instruction amenable to change and improvement. This is as true in black inner city schools as in the more affluent white suburbs. Nevertheless, we do not claim here that every child's reading problem can be solved and that every class, no matter how difficult its composition, can be readily taught; for even though the range of abilities and of instruction was very wide in this study, we can easily imagine conditions more intractable than those we found.

While we believe that our general formulation of school organization applies to much more than the first grade, there are nevertheless peculiarities of first grade reading instruction that do not characterize other subjects and later grades. First grade reading instruction is in varying degrees based on letter, word, and short story, and it proceeds in small, steady progressions. That format lends itself to being conceptualized and measured as amount of material covered. Other formats based upon larger and more complex units of material spanning longer time intervals do not lend themselves as readily to such conceptual treatment. In addition, first grade reading characteristically employs reading groups to deal with the diversity of children's abilities. Later grades must cope with as great if not greater diversity, yet reading groups of the type used in first grade tend to be used less frequently and may not be used at all. Other solutions to the problem of classroom diversity must then be sought. Finally, first grade represents the first serious encounter by most children with the regime of schooling. They arrive at school without knowing its ins and outs, without having experienced its seamier and more destructive sides; they appear willing at their young age to give teachers the benefit of doubts they develop later on. In the later grades, when children have become more sophisticated and cynical about school, when some have experienced failure and disillusionment, and when the weakness of the school at keeping order has been made manifest to them, the agenda of the classroom teacher becomes more preoccupied with order and discipline than appears to be the case in the first grade.

What, then, about the power of the formulation developed in this study? Is it not parochially tied to the particulars of the first grade and inapplicable to other grades? We think not. Our perspective on school organization and its workings is in fact based upon general problems of schooling—dealing with the diversity of students, allocation of time, and use of materials—which occur at all grades. What differs from grade to grade is the particular set of solutions available to cope with these problems. First grade is but the first in a progression of grades with both similarities and differences in solutions, and subsequent investigations will have to indicate what they are.

Like all studies that entail fieldwork and analysis extending over long spans of time, this one has depended on the goodwill and at times extraordinary efforts of many people. By an unfair yet understandable convention, those who make the most essential contribution—the principals, teachers, and first graders who allowed the study to take place—are alas promised anonymity, and as a result cannot have their contribution publicly acknowledged. But we thank them nevertheless.

We owe a great debt to a number of graduate students in the Department of Education at the University of Chicago who in 1969 and 1970 assisted Rebecca Barr with the collection and preparation of data for her investigation of reading readiness, instruction, and learning: Lyn Bortnick, Nancy Feaman, Mary Jane Kibby, Michael Kibby, Genevieve Lopardo, Katherine Morsbach, Susan Snyder, and Joan Staples. Michael Kibby was also instrumental in developing the measure of reading readiness. The high quality and completeness of the data are testimony to the care and thoroughness of their work. We express our thanks.

In the course of time, we had opportunities to return to this material, rethink it, and reanalyze it. Our efforts were encouraged by the Educational Finance and Productivity Center at the University of Chicago, directed by Charles E. Bidwell and Douglas M. Windham. The Center, and through it, our work, was supported by the National Institute of Education under contract 400-77-0094. We express our gratitude to our colleagues in the Center and to Michael Cohen and Virginia Koehler of NIE.

We benefited from the observations of Charles Bidwell and Lee Shulman, who graciously plowed through some uncommonly dense prose in earlier drafts of several chapters; the book is better for their suffering. Thomas Mendrala, with his meticulous reading of the text and tables, found several inexcusable errors and helped us to restore both the manuscript and our equanimity. And we were rescued on more than one occasion by the statistical wisdom of Larry Hedges and David Rogosa. Whether we ultimately survive statistically is not their problem. Wayne Levy helped us numerous times with computer analyses, as did Rose Chen with her proofreading, and Yvette Courtade and Westina Matthews assisted with the typing of earlier drafts. We also thank Therese Chappell, who typed the final draft of the complete manuscript, and Adam Gamoran, who prepared the index.

We owe an extraordinary debt to Nonglak Wiratchai, who while completing her own dissertation on an unrelated topic faithfully carried the whole burden of the computer analysis. Her work was impeccable. She did it with great cheerfulness and frequently anticipated what we would need before we could ask her. There is no adequate acknowledgment; including her name on the title page signifies only part of what we owe her.

1. Introduction

Over the past quarter century, the civil rights movement, the Great Society programs, and the more recent rise of public sentiment for accountability, minimum competency, and free choice have all indicated deficiencies in how well the schools perform and have sought remedies for them through legislation, judicial action, and other political means. Yet it is a remarkable commentary on the state of our knowledge about education that despite the staggering sums invested and the massive efforts to improve and reform the schools, we do not have a clear conception of how they work. This book is an effort to find out precisely that: how schools work. Like any organization that tries to produce something of value, schools attract, allocate, and mobilize resources; and while we know a lot about how the amounts of different sorts of resources are associated with learning—the value that schools are supposed to produce—we do not know much about how the different parts of an educational system contribute or about how resources are actually used to produce the value.

We will show in the course of this volume that when school systems are analyzed in the fashion we describe here, some extraordinarily large educational effects appear in places where they have not hitherto been sought. For example, in the past, where comparisons between school

1

characteristics have shown exceedingly modest effects upon learning, and comparisons between classrooms both modest and inconsistent ones, we have found strikingly large effects on learning that originate in activities taking place in the suborganization of classrooms: in reading groups. Our evidence suggests that the differences between groups that account for so much learning get averaged out in classroom and school comparisons and as a result the productive events taking place inside schools become obscured. Does this mean, then, that classrooms produce only trivial effects? Not at all. Classroom characteristics might not affect individual learning directly, but rather influence the formation of instructional groups. Group arrangements, not learning, may then be thought of as the value produced by classrooms.

This book is written according to the premise that our unsatisfactory understanding of how schools work and what they produce should be attributed primarily to the lack of an adequate general formulation of school production. Past work has been largely preoccupied with trying to account for differences in individual learning by associating them with district, school, and classroom characteristics. But this general strategy does not address the question of workings directly. Rather, such familiar measures as per pupil expenditure, class size, teacher experience and credentials, the availability of laboratories and libraries—the staples of educational effectiveness research—are little more than remote proxies for the productive activities taking place in educational institutions. How much money there is is one question; how it is spent, quite another. The library may have thousands of volumes; but are they checked out and read? Some teachers may be verbally facile but so inept at managing a class that not enough time is left for them to turn their verbal intelligence into sound instruction. Teachers in the early primary grades usually divide their classes into reading groups; but knowing that students are assigned to a group does not indicate the nature of the group instruction they receive. In all these cases, the productive events that constitute schooling escape both conceptualization and consideration.

Our formulation begins with the idea that school systems are organizations that like others can be readily subject to sociological analysis. In all organizations labor is divided, which means that different activities are carried out in the different parts and that the parts are connected to each other in a coherent way. The parts of school systems are very familiar. They consist of a central administration with jurisdiction over a school district as well as local administrations situated in each school with responsibility for what happens therein. The business of schooling, mainly instruction, takes place in classrooms run by teachers; and teachers preside not only over classes but over parts of them as well when they rely upon grouped forms of instruction. We will show how the work that gets done in district offices, schools, classes, and instructional groups is different in character, that these separate jurisdictions are locations for carrying on different sorts of activities. Indeed, this proposition is true for teachers as classroom instructors and as group instructors in that teachers do different things in organizing a class from what they do while instructing subgroups within it. Part of the answer to our question of how schools work, then, is to be found by identifying the distinct events happening at each level of school system organization.

A second part of the answer can be found by discovering how the events characteristic of one level influence those taking place at another. It would be a strange organization indeed if the parts were hermetically sealed off from each other; if, for example, what the principal did had no bearing on what teachers did and if what teachers did made no difference for what students did and learned. Yet it is precisely the failure to come up with satisfactory answers to these questions that has caused so much grief in our understanding of educational effects. The answer must come from identifying correctly what the activities are and from being able to trace their antecedents and effects across pathways that connect one level to another.

The third part of the answer pertains not so much to what to look for as it does to how to look for it. School systems, like other forms of social existence, are characterized by variability. We can learn about their workings by attending to the different ways that comparable parts act: different schools in the same system, different classes in the same school, different groups in the same class. What can vary in these levels of school organization is the way in which resources are allocated, transformed, and used. A particular resource, like books, may be purchased by the district office. All fourth grade mathematics texts, for example, can then be distributed to each elementary school, thence to be stocked in each fourth grade class. Thus, a simple process of resource transmission takes place. From there, teachers in the same school may use the text in almost identical ways or in vastly different ways depending on how they organize their instructional programs. The program itself determines the instructional use, and hence the meaning, of the resource. Accordingly, insofar as the school is no more than a transmission belt for transporting books from the district office to the classroom, school-by-school comparisons will show similar activities. Class-by-class comparisons in textbook use, however, might show sharp contrasts. Depending upon the nature of those class contrasts, they may average out to show no school differences or bunch up to show marked school differences. In either case, it is the comparison of events at the same level—school and class in these examples—that tells us what is going on. We will try to discover how schools work, then, by identifying the ways in which resources are used at each level of school system organization, by tracing the effects of events from one level to another, and by comparing events both within and between parts of the organization.

NATURE OF INQUIRY

The primary purpose of this book is to develop a formulation about how schools and school systems work, with particular emphasis on classroom instruction. Like most reports that treat both concepts and data, this one also constitutes a polite fiction by presenting ideas in a coherent fashion when in fact the work at times proceeded by thinking back and forth between concepts and data in a less than orderly way. Our thinking was informed by two sources. First, it was informed by concepts drawn mainly from the field of sociology. We view the work as a study in the sociology of organizations concerned with matters of social structure, of how work in educational organizations gets divided and performed, and of how resources get allocated and used.

Second, our formulative efforts were supported by a review of the extant literature concerned with schooling effects and by a secondary analysis of empirical data on first grade reading instruction. Sociological and economic studies of schooling effects and psychological and educational investigations of classroom instruction were analyzed and codified to determine what is known about educational effects and the organization of their production. The secondary analysis of an existing set of data provided the opportunity to test some of our hunches about how schools work. These data, derived from a study of reading instruction in fifteen first grade classes, allowed us to explore the organization of classroom instruction: the social grouping of children for instruction, the design of instruction for reading groups, and the learning of individual children.

We have tried here to rethink the problem of educational effects to determine whether the doleful conclusions that many previous studies have drawn about the effectiveness of schooling are justified. Our strategy has not been to devise new measurement and statistical techniques or to test hypotheses in the conventional sense. Rather, it has been directed primarily at recasting the ways in which educational effects have been conceptualized. Hence our preoccupation with questions of formulation. The analysis of empirical data, accordingly, has served primarily a generative function to help us discover how to think about the nature of school system organization, of schooling and their effects.

THE FORMULATION

Levels of Organization

Labor in school systems is divided; it is differentiated by task into different organizational levels in a hierarchical arrangement. While we

customarily think about hierarchies as pertaining to relations of authority, rank, and power, they not only are manifestations of stratification
and status distinction, but also represent organizational differentiation,
a manifestation of labor being specialized and other resources distributed
to different locations, of the elements of production having been both
separated and tied together in some workable arrangement. We are
concerned here with hierarchy in this latter sense.

In an educational division of labor, school systems comprise
several levels of administrative and staff officers as well as "production" workers occupying positions with district, school, and classroom
jurisdictions. In addition, school systems are differentiated according to
the resources they use, such as time and physical objects—like books—
that constitute instructional materials. As we shall indicate shortly, time
is a resource that has meaning at all levels of the hierarchy, but its
meaning has different manifestations at each level. Textbooks, by contrast, are productive resources only inside classrooms. School systems
also contain one additional element: students who are both the clients
of the organization, the intended beneficiaries of its services, and, because schools are engaged in effecting change in children, productive
resources in their own right because they participate directly and actively
in their own learning.

When organizations are differentiated, it is because their parts make
distinct contributions to the overall productive enterprise. This means
that people located hierarchically at different places perform different
kinds of activities; it also means that resources come into play in different
ways depending upon where they are utilized in the productive process.
A complete formulation of school production, therefore, should identify
all relevant combinations of people, time, and material resources at each
hierarchical level.

More specifically, school systems characteristically contain a managerial component responsible for centralized financial, personnel, procurement, plant maintenance, and supervisory functions applicable to
all their constituent elements. This component is also engaged in direct
dealings with agencies of the federal and state governments as well as
with locally based interest groups and units of municipal government.
Activities occurring at this managerial level have *nothing directly* to do
with running schools or teaching students but rather are concerned with
the acquisition of resources, with general supervision, and with the
maintenance of relations with the surrounding community including
suppliers of labor. We refer to this as the *district* level of organization;
its jurisdiction includes all schools in the district.

Even though districts are divided into levels (elementary and secondary) related to the ages of students, and some are also divided into
geographical areas as well as functional units, we are primarily con-

cerned—at the next lower hierarchical level—with *schools*. Contrary to conventional belief, schools are not organizational units of instruction. They are structures akin to switching yards where children within a given age range and from a designated geographical area are assigned to teachers who bring them into contact with approved learning materials, specified as being appropriate to age or ability, during certain allotted periods of time. Schools deal in potentialities; they assemble a supply of teachers, of students, and of resources over a given period of time. Their central activities are the assignment of children to specific teachers, the allocation of learning materials to classrooms, the arrangement of a schedule so that all children in the school can be allotted an appropriate amount of time to spend on subjects in the curriculum, and the integration of grades so that work completed in one represents adequate preparation for the next.

These activities are the primary responsibility of school principals; they are core functions peculiar to the school level of organization. This is so because decisions affecting the fate of all classrooms in a school are not likely to be left to individuals (teachers) who have in mind primarily classroom interests rather than whole school interests and whose self-interest puts them in a poor position to settle disputes among equals. Nor are they likely to be left to district-wide administrators, whose locations can be too remote and jurisdictions too widespread to allow them to make informed decisions about local school events.

While these decisions constitute the peculiar core activities of school level administration, they by no means exhaust the responsibilities of school administrators, which frequently include such matters as planning curriculum; establishing disciplinary standards; and making school policies for homework, decorum in public places, and the like. But while such concerns are frequently characteristic of school administration, they are not peculiar to it because district-wide administrators and teachers also participate in them at the school level in fulfilling responsibilities within their own respective jurisdictions.

While instruction is not the business of the school, it is the business of *classrooms* and of teachers responsible for the direct engagement of students in learning activities. Aggregations of children are assigned to specific teachers who direct their activities and bring them into immediate contact with various sorts of learning materials. These activities are more than potentialities because children's active engagement working with teachers and materials is what enables them to learn.

Because classes contain diverse aggregations of children, it is not automatic that the instruction appropriate for one member of the aggregation will be appropriate for another. Hence, teachers in the lower grades characteristically create an additional level of suborganization to manage activities not easily handled in a grouping as large as the class.

For example, in primary grade reading, there are suborganizations called *instructional groups* that represent still another level of organizational differentiation.

Finally, there are *individual students*. It is only individuals who work on tasks, and it is only they who learn; so that while work tasks might be set for all students in the class or in a group, the individual members vary in how much work they do and in how much they learn.

We argue here not only that school systems can be described by their constituent organizational levels, but that the events, activities, and organizational forms found at each level should be seen as addressing distinct as well as partially overlapping agendas. Districts, schools, classes, and instructional groups are structurally differentiated from each other; and what is more they make different contributions to the overall operation of the school system.

While the empirical investigation reported in this book concerns the first elementary school grade, we recognize that not all schools have precisely the same organizational pattern. In the upper elementary grades, for example, formalized instructional groups characteristically used for primary level reading might or might not be employed; and in secondary schools, which lack self-contained classrooms, a departmental level of organization usually appears as does formal tracking that distinguishes students largely on the basis of ability within schools but not within classes. Despite these variations, the general principle of differentiated structures and agendas holds.

Linkages between Levels

If organizational levels are as distinct as this analysis suggests, how is it possible to think about a coherent production process for the whole school district organization? How should the connections between levels be formulated? We contend that each level of a school system has its own core productive agenda even though certain activities are performed at more than one level. That is, productive events of differing character occur at each level to effect outcomes that are themselves characteristic of each level. For example, a school outcome becomes a productive condition in classes yielding in turn a class outcome; the class outcome in turn becomes a productive element for instructional groups yielding a group outcome; and so on. We see, then, a set of nested hierarchical layers, each having a conditional and contributory relation to events and outcomes occurring at adjacent ones.

Consider an example of how levels of organization are connected to each other to constitute school production. As we observed earlier, classroom characteristics do not directly affect individual learning; they influence the formation of instructional groups. This might seem to be a strange statement since everyone knows that classroom teachers are responsible for instructing all children in a class. However, the teacher's job, we maintain, is first to transform an aggregation of children into an arrangement suitable for establishing an instructional program. In first grade reading, this usually means creating instructional reading groups. Hence, before any instruction takes place, decisions are made about how to arrange the class; whether to teach everyone together in one group, as in recitation; whether to establish subgroups in which only some children work intensively with the teacher while the others proceed by themselves with little supervision; whether to set everyone to work independently at their desks to perform at their own rate such more or less individualized tasks as are contained in workbooks.

The results of these classroom decisions are not instructional, nor do they appear as individual learning. They are alternative grouping arrangements which should be thought of as class outcomes, or values. We must draw a distinction between what teachers do in organizing classes *for* instruction and the instruction they actually provide for the groupings of children that make up classroom organization. Down the road, those grouping arrangements influence individual learning through a chain of connections consisting of instructional activities. Individual learning, however, is not itself a class outcome. As our story unfolds, we will show how class grouping arrangements determine certain characteristics of the groups composing them, in particular the level of children's ability characteristic of each classroom group. As it turns out, this level of ability is a direct determinant of certain instructional activities undertaken by teachers, who treat differently composed groups in different ways. One form this treatment takes is the amount of material covered, which we construe as an outcome, or value, created by instructional groups. (Note again: individual learning is not a group outcome any more than it is a class outcome.) Then, depending on how much material children cover over a given span of time, in combination with their own characteristics, they learn proportionally more or less. In sum, group arrangements are the value created at the class level, coverage the value at the group level, and learning the value at the individual level. Note particularly that the activities and outcomes characteristic of each level are qualitatively distinct—grouping, coverage, learning—and that they are linked together in a coherent manner.

Most readers will have recognized that we have been describing aspects of the familiar phenomenon of ability grouping, but not in a familiar way. Instead of simply distinguishing students according to whether they belong to homogeneous or heterogeneous groups, which is the usual (and not very illuminating) way of studying grouping, we have tried to identify distinct though related activities that refer to sets of decisions that constitute class organization, grouped instruction, and individual learning.

This brief analysis shows the concatenation of distinct activities that constitute and surround classroom instruction. An implication of this analysis is that we can take any single educationally relevant resource and trace its manifestations across several hierarchical levels of school system organization. In chapter 3, we will do just that for the important resource of student aptitude for reading (reading readiness among first graders). But to illustrate the logic of the formulation, we will consider here the resource of time.

A school district administration makes three kinds of decisions about time. The first reveals its responsibilities of law enforcement to the state: the schools must remain open for a stipulated number of days to qualify for state aid. While this enforcement of state law places an outside limit on time available for teaching, it does not bear directly on teaching, instruction, or learning. Furthermore, when the length of the academic year is combined with a determination about the length of the school day, the second type of district decision is made: how much time teachers (and other employees) will work as part of a contractual agreement with suppliers of labor. The third type of decision pertains to when the schools will start and finish each academic year, open and close each day, and recess for vacations, decisions that determine when and whether parents can leave the household for work and arrange for the care of very young children. Basic time considerations, then, at the district level of organization are tied up with law enforcement, labor contracts, and the integration of the school system with households in the community; and district outcomes can be defined in these terms.

School systems, of course, do not hire teachers in general, but teachers who instruct in particular subjects in secondary schools and in a variety of basic skills in elementary schools. Hiring teachers by subject and skill presumes that curricular priorities have been established, which means that decisions have been made about how much time will be devoted to each segment of the curriculum: to English, mathematics, science, foreign languages, and so on, in secondary schools; to reading, arithmetic, science, social studies, and so on, in elementary schools. At the level of schools, these decisions become manifest in the time schedule, a formal statement written in fine-grained time units of how much time will be devoted to each subject matter and to extracurricular pursuits.

The school schedule is really a political document that acknowledges the influences of administrative directives and the preferences of teachers and parents expressing varying views about the welfare of the student body, of individual students, and of different types of students. It embodies past decisions about how much ordinary instruction there will be, in which subjects, at which more or less desirable times, and in which more or less desirable places. It expresses how segregated or desegregated classes will be in response to higher level administrative directives as well as the integration of the handicapped in regular and special classes. These resultant priorities conventionally expressed in the time schedule are an outcome of school level organization.

The curricular priorities expressed in the school time schedule represent temporal constraints upon the work of teachers in classrooms. While in secondary schools the order of classes throughout the day is established by the schedule itself, in elementary schools the teachers themselves arrange activities within the confines of daily time allotments, deciding which activities come earliest in the day, which next, and which last, with some flexibility about how long each successive activity will last. In addition to determining which activities take place during the "better" and "worse" times of the day, teachers also establish, within school guidelines and across parts of the curriculum (reading, arithmetic, science), how long instruction will last in each of a variety of classroom formats (whole class, grouped, individual instruction) and how much time gets wasted through interruptions, poor planning, and transitions between activities. At the classroom level, then, teachers allocate time in ways that bear directly upon instruction by determining the amount of time that students will have available for productive work in various subject areas.

Finally, given the time that teachers make available for productive work, students then decide how much of that time to use and to waste, and in so doing influence the amount they will learn.

What we have done here is to trace the allocation of time through the layers of school system organization to show how it takes on different manifestations as district, school, class, and individual phenomena. We have also shown how the nature of time at one level becomes a time condition for events occurring at the next lower level.

What our formulation does is very simple. It locates productive activities at all levels of the school system that in more common but less precise parlance are known as administration and teaching. It also states that productive activities specific to levels produce outcomes specific to levels. Accordingly, we distinguish carefully between the productive processes that constitute the working of school organization from the outcomes, or values, produced by those processes. They are not the same thing, although they have commonly been confused in discussions about educational effects. The distinction between production and value not only is important conceptually, but provides a principle that ties the parts of the levels of school organization into a coherent pattern.

The formulation also carries us some distance in thinking about how the effectiveness of schools should be viewed. The common practice of using individual achievement (or aggregations of individual achievement) as a primary index to gauge whether schools are productive is of limited value because there are other outcomes that are the direct result of productive processes occurring at higher levels of school system organization. There is no question that achievement is an important outcome at the individual level; it may or may not be an important outcome at other levels, as our previous analyses of time and grouping indicate. Perhaps, for example, the properly understood outcome of instructional groups is a group-specific rate of covering learning materials or the amount of time a teacher makes available for instruction, outcomes that when considered at the individual level are properly construed as conditions of learning. An important class level outcome may be the creation of an appropriate grouping arrangement or the establishment of a productive time schedule, both of which are conditions bearing on the nature of group instruction. We will consider both of these possibilities in later chapters.

Similarly, at the school level, the important outcomes may be the allocation of time to curricular areas that makes enough time available for basic skill subjects, an assignment of teachers to classes that makes the most appropriate use of their talents or that provides equitable work loads, or the appropriate coordination of skill subjects from year to year so that children are prepared for the work of the succeeding grade. At the district level, perhaps negotiating labor contracts that satisfy employees, administrators, and the taxpayers, or having a satisfactory book and materials procurement policy represent significant outcomes.

As we indicated earlier and must emphasize again, this book is designed primarily to reformulate current ideas about how school organizations work to produce a variety of values, only one of which is the learning of individual students. We have undertaken this task in two ways: first, by assessing analytically the extant knowledge on educational effects and classroom instruction; and second, by trying our ideas out on a body of data, appropriate to this task even though collected earlier for different purposes. Chapter 2 contains our reanalysis of prevalent views about the effects of schooling and instruction leading to the derivation of our own formulation of how schools work. Chapter 3 presents an empirical introduction to our views about organizational levels and the connections between them. The next three chapters contain detailed treatments of productive activities occurring in classrooms: chapter 4 examines how classes become reorganized into reading groups, chapter 5 focuses on the design of instruction for different groups, and chapter 6 explores how instructional conditions, particularly the content covered, influence learning to read. We close in the final chapter with a summary and a statement of implications for some perennial and controversial issues in public educational policy. We should add here that chapter 2 assumes a familiarity with specialized bodies of literature. The reader can safely proceed to chapter three.

2. Considering and Reconsidering Educational Effects

The study of educational organization and its effects has in recent years become a small industry occupied with how educative efforts influence learning. Our work is about what it means to produce educational effects, and in this chapter we explain our perspective on that question and its derivation from the major prevailing approaches. That derivation will show the continuities between our work and what has been done before and the ways in which it represents a distinct departure. We make no claim to have cited every pertinent study, only to have presented the predominant perspectives and approaches.

The study of educational production has been vexed for many reasons not least of which is that disciplinary boundaries have separated investigators working on different facets of the same problems. A barrier has stood between sociology and economics, on the one hand, and psychology, on the other. It has effectively restricted communication between those who study teaching and instruction and those who study schools, districts, and individual careers. Differences in judgment about whether educational effects should be determined at the level of individuals or at some level of school organization have also divided investigators. We will argue here that disciplinary boundaries are conceptually artificial, and that the search for the most appropriate level of analysis is misdirected because schooling involves all parts of a school system.

In the pages to follow, we address the predominant formulations of educational effects to show how they are controversial and to identify their confusing areas of conceptual overlap. There are no conventional names consistently given to these major approaches, and for that reason we use designations intended to evoke certain distinctive lines of investigation. These are: school production, status attainment, teaching effectiveness, and instructional time. We begin with the first.

SOCIOLOGICAL AND ECONOMIC APPROACHES

School Production

School production is a useful designation that relates the workings of schools to individual learning. Analyses of school production have been most characteristically carried out by using the economists' formulation of the production function. According to Lau, "An educational production function relates the levels of identifiable educational outcomes to the qualities of identifiable educational inputs. It is fundamentally a microeconomic concept, designed to apply at the level of an individual student" (1979, p. 33), although it can be expressed for aggregations of individuals as well. At the same time, Lau indicates the importance of identifying "the technological relation between educational outputs and inputs" (p. 34). In these two statements, he has identified perhaps the most persistent concerns in research on educational effects. Yet a conceptual problem arises: Where does the productive work of schooling occur? Lau might mean that the technology resides in an educational organization (a school), and not in the individual, this despite the fact that he locates the production function at the level of individual students. Then again, perhaps not; maybe the technology does reside in the individual student as producer.

The difficulty here is that production function analysis does not directly address problems of educational technology, that is, the organization of the factors of educational production. It proceeds by compiling a plausible list of educational resources and determining their marginal contribution to some outcome, usually achievement. When this is done, one is left to assume that the resources, whose availability but not whose use is known, when added up constitute the operating technology. This might be a more tenable assumption for industrial organizations than for educational ones, for in the former much is known about workable combinations of productive factors, and much of the technology might be built into machinery of known capacity. Not so in the latter (as well as in other labor-intensive and people-serving organizations), where the questions of what is the technology, how is it organized, and what are the effects it has, are open. The educational researcher, then, is in the awkward position of trying to identify the technology in the first place and at the same time chart its effects. A tall order.

For the most part, production function analysis assumes what we really need to know: how school systems are organized and how they work. This is the gist of the observation by Averch and his colleagues about input-output analysis: "The school in which the student is enrolled affects his outcome only to the extent that it serves as the channel through which resources flow to him. In particular, the structure and organization of the school and classroom are neglected" (1972, p. 31). The channel metaphor expresses well the idea implicit in production function analysis that the school is simply a conduit through which available resources flow.

Aside from whether the nature of technology is adequately taken into account by conventional studies of school production, there are additional confusions about whether the productive unit is the firm (such as the school district, the school, the classroom) having organized productive capacities, or the individual student, the technological agent working within an organizational setting which supplies resources. The latter construction gains support from economists such as Lau (1979, p. 43) and Murnane (1975, p. 6) who maintain that the lack of a learning theory retards the study of educational production. If production resides fundamentally in an organizational setting, then a learning theory—a technological statement that applies to individuals—is of limited value. If an organization is the fundamental productive unit, then we need to know how it produces.

Despite conceptual confusions about where the technology actually resides, particular studies of school production indicate that production takes place in educational organizations and at different levels within them. For example, some studies deal with the properties of districts (Bidwell and Kasarda 1975; Brown and Saks 1975; Katzman 1971); of schools (Brookover et al. 1979; Burkhead, Fox, and Holland 1967; Coleman et al. 1966; McDill and Rigsby 1973; Rutter et al. 1979); and of classrooms (Barr 1973–74; Murnane 1975; Summers and Wolfe 1977; Thomas 1977). By and large, they try to discover properties at one or another level of school organization (in the context of community and individual background characteristics) that produce learning (or achievement). Along these lines, we find a distinct trend in this work since the Coleman report of 1966 toward the identification of technological processes. The work of Bidwell and Kasarda (1975), Brown and Saks (1980), and Summers and Wolfe (1974) is particularly important in this respect. They address themselves more to the use of resources in districts, schools, and classrooms in a technological sense that makes a difference in pupil learning than to the mere availability of resources at those levels without regard to their use.

Individuals represent both the raw materials of such production and its beneficiaries. The material (individuals) enters the process "raw"; its state is then changed by virtue of productive activities occurring in the organization. Individuals do not appear in this formulation to be the primary productive units. Obviously, however, they contribute to their own learning through their efforts and activities; and there is a sense in which they are mentally productive. The latter is the kind of production that interests instructional and cognitive psychologists, though how the functioning of the mind is related to the functioning of educational organizations remains a mystery whose solution is not likely to be found by confusing the different sorts of production and where each occurs.

The views of researchers on the location and nature of educational production have direct implications for the organizational levels at which empirical evidence is gathered and organized. For example, both Lau and Murnane maintain that data for the study of educational production should be collected at the individual level. Consider a statement by Lau: "Data can be available at the level of the individual student, class, grade, school, school district, metropolitan area, or state. The degree of aggregation of the data is not necessarily the same on the output side and on the input side . . . Of course, ideally one seeks data at the individual student level when possible" (1979, p. 40).

This contention, however, does not go without dissent. Bidwell and Kasarda (1975), for example, have identified certain productive events that occur and should be formulated at the district level, such as the extraction of valuable resources from the community and other levels of government and their subsequent allocation to lower level units of district organization (schools and classrooms in particular). These extractive functions are not properly illuminated when data are treated at the individual level because they represent district activities.

In our view, the principal characteristic of school production research is its concern with what properties of school organization create increments of learning. And while we place great emphasis on the importance of understanding how individual learning is fostered, that problem does not exhaust the investigation of educational production. A critical part of the production question, however, is how school organizations work; that is, what is the nature of their internal operation that makes them productive? This question requires investigating educational organizations at their various levels as well as the nature of the connections between the levels. Accordingly, to establish how district extractions of resources from the environment are redistributed at lower levels of the school system is no less a problem in educational production than to establish how teaching methods are related to individual learning. A complete picture of educational production necessarily includes how the workings of educational organizations at all levels contribute to producing increments of learning in individuals. But that complete picture cannot be drawn by restricting attention to events specified only to the individual level, or indeed to any other single level.

The influence of schooling on individuals has been the focus of a different but closely related branch of research on educational effects: the study of status attainment. The differences between school production and status attainment research are subtle but fundamental. As indicated above, the former is concerned with identifying those properties of educational organizations that affect individual outcomes. The emphasis is on the organization. The latter is concerned with the outcomes and the experiences of individuals that lead to these outcomes. To understand the differences between the two, we first consider the varieties of work that fall into the status attainment category. We then contrast status attainment with school production research.

Status Attainment

Some of the earliest explorations of status attainment are found in the work of Kahl (1953), Parsons (1959), Sibley (1942), and Stouffer (1962), all of whom tried to account for variations in individuals' educational and occupational aspirations on the basis of variations in social class position and schooling. After the 1940s and 1950s, when serious work on these topics began, the potentialities for the elaboration of the rather simple social class explanations for aspiration were recognized. In the 1960s, both the rapid expansion and formalization of what attainment meant (beyond aspiration) and what its causes and conditions might be proceeded apace. The major treatise of the 1960s was Blau and Duncan's *The American Occupational Structure* (1967), even though the work of Sewell and his colleagues (1957) as well as that of others had been well under way. The contribution of these works was to establish the centrality of educational events to the understanding of social stratification and mobility and to establish the importance of explaining variations in individual attainments according to variations in school experiences among other causes. This latter set of concerns, as we shall see, became one of the variant forms of examining educational effects.

The "basic model" of Blau and Duncan (1967, pp. 165–71) was designed to explain variation in the occupational status of adult males according to the status of first job, amount of education, and fathers' occupational and educational status. Hindsight shows how this and the parallel early work of Sewell and his colleagues set the future agenda. It reinforced the importance of individual status based upon family of orientation, it established the importance of the amount of schooling, and it treated both the long- and short-term effects of education on placement in the labor market.

It is a short conceptual step to realize that adult earnings, for example, are as much an indication of attainment as occupational status, both in the near and in the long terms; and not surprisingly, both economists and sociologists have investigated these forms of attainment (Alexander, Eckland, and Griffin 1975; Fägerlind 1975; Haller and Portes 1973; Sewell and Hauser 1975; Taubman and Wales 1974). It is also clear that the attainment of a given economic and social level can be attributed to similar conditions, most particularly background characteristics (such as socioeconomic status), individual endowments (such as intelligence), and social involvements, all of which represent different amounts of human resources and advantage negotiable into career advancements.

Several observers (Bowman 1976; Sewell, Hauser, and Featherman 1976) have appropriately claimed that studies of this kind are really investigations of individual careers, of individual life-cycles. Certain kinds of *individual* characteristics and experiences such as original home background, ability, schooling, and interaction with people are shown to be important influences on occupational choice and long-term life chances. Strictly speaking, these are not primarily studies of school effects even though the impact of the amount of schooling is usually weighed in along with the effects of other influences upon career decision making or the acquisition of human capital. These studies aim primarily at identifying the processes entailed in the transmission of status in the form of earnings and occupational prestige from generation to generation.

Status transmission is not simply a matter of individual characteristics and their changes over time, and in view of that, recent investigators have drawn attention to the importance of certain elements of social structure as mechanisms of status transmission. Among these elements of structure are the network of significant others (noted above) and certain characteristics of schools, primary among which is tracking. Through a series of investigations, Alexander, Cook, and McDill (1978), Alexander and McDill (1976), Alexander and Eckland (1975a), Heyns (1974), and Rosenbaum (1976) identify conditions surrounding the assignment of secondary school students to curriculum groups (tracks) and show how track membership contributes to the attainment of status. Tracking in this line of work elaborates the meaning of "school" or "schooling" in status attainment models beyond the simple preoccupation with amount of schooling. Recent work, then, on status attainment has begun to consider what characteristics of schools, or events that occur inside them, influence status attainment. Along these lines, we find the inclusion of additional school characteristics beyond tracking: for example, teacher characteristics (experience and credentials) and school resources (books and expenditures) reported in the work of Sørenson and Hallinan (1977).

At this point, one is entitled to feel confused about what is happening conceptually; or perhaps we have brought confusion upon ourselves by making a distinction between school production and status attainment in the first place. Consider the work of Alexander and Eckland (1975a). In a model designed to account for educational as well as occupational attainment in the near and far term, these writers include the sophomore and senior year curriculum (track) placement of each student. In other studies that include tracking, we find new meanings attached to attainment as well as to school and schooling. Attainment in Alexander and McDill (1976) refers to high school mathematics achievement, to senior class rank, and to several measures of self-concept. Alexander, Cook, and McDill (1978) extend the meaning of attainment to include several measures of school achievement (senior year), as well as application to and acceptance by a college. In sum, status attainments extend not only into the realm of adult life chances but also to very near-term secondary and pre-tertiary school accomplishments. This construction of attainments over time, of course, is nothing new. It appears in Heyns's (1974) work on tracking, which treats the effects of curriculum placement on grades and aspirations in a model that includes social class background, ability, and number of siblings. It also appears in Sørenson and Hallinan's (1977) work, which deals with achievement. But interestingly enough, even though Sørensen and Hallinan's formulation pertains to status attainment, they present it as a formulation of school effects.

The term "school effects" does not clarify things conceptually at all. This term comes close to expressing the same sorts of concerns that school production models deal with. Sørensen and Hallinan, however, add to the terminological confusion by claiming to be concerned with the process of learning, "the learning of intellectual knowledge and skills that schools try to teach and test for in academic achievement tests" (1977, p. 275). But, in fact, they are concerned with how schools make opportunities available by means of which children can learn through the behavior of teachers, curriculum, teacher characteristics, and school resources discussed earlier; and in particular, with how these school properties can be appropriately expressed in a model of school effects. In sum, the domains of the individual and of the school remain only vaguely distinguished.

A much less confusing formulation is found in Alwin and Otto, who deal with school effects in the light of school context. Their formulation is intended "to spell out the critical factors operating within- and between-schools which produce variation in college plans and occupational aspirations" (1977, p. 262). They go on to state that "the within-school part of the model is similar to the Wisconsin model [of individual status attainment] for educational and occupational achievement" (p. 262) and that "in addition to the . . . within-school factors our model incorporates three contextual variables—average socioeconomic status, average student ability, and the proportion of the enrollment that is male" (p. 264). The contextual elements in this model represent the school effects (or school production) component while the variety of individual and background characteristics represent its status attainment component.

The work of Alwin and Otto is part of a larger body of research that treats the social context of schools (Alexander and Eckland 1975b; Brookover et al. 1979; Hauser 1970; Wilson 1959; the literature is reviewed extensively by Burstein 1980). Here we find that the nature of school organization is derived by summing (or aggregating) such characteristics of individual students as aptitude, socioeconomic status, and sex to the school (or other) level of organization in order to provide an indication of its climate of values or its general social ambience. Aside from the interpretive difficulties that such aggregating procedures create, they provide at best a measure of a school's atmosphere—is it predominantly working class in composition, is it racially mixed or segregated, are there many more girls than boys?—but little about the "critical factors operating" or a sense about how a school works. A case in point is the Brookover et al. (1979) study of school composition and climate. Teacher and student characteristics are aggregated to the school level along with structural properties, like differentiation, and treated additively as determinants of school achievement. This formulation does not countenance the possibility that teachers might "deal with" the aggregate characteristics of students in classrooms rather than in the school as a whole by differentiating instructional arrangements and activities. For this reason, the study does not really treat the workings of the school; because of its concentration solely on the school level of analysis, it cannot explore more generally the question of where organizational differentiation might take place.

This is not to deny the importance of school climate; it simply indicates that measures of climate do not by themselves provide a picture of school operation. Studies of climate, however, do indeed fasten upon what we believe to be a crucial aspect of educational organization: the distributional properties of school systems and of their parts. Their limitation is that they stop at establishing direct connections between context and outcomes without taking the next step of inquiring how the organization deals with these distributions of children and the problems they pose for the school's productive activities.

The distinction between work that treats the characteristics of schools and work that examines the intergenerational linkages that influence attainments of status has become conceptually blurred. It appears that studies of status attainment and of school production examine basically the same set of events but differ primarily in emphasis. They vary first in the particular achievements and attainments in question and in whether those achievements appear in the very near term, such as educational aspiration, achievement, or class rank; in the very far term, such as occupational status or earnings after the first job; or at some time in between. They vary second in the component of the status transmission process singled out for particular attention, such as parental background, patterns of social interaction, school characteristics, and individual characteristics like ability. Third, the school itself as an influence upon outcomes is treated differently depending upon whether long- or short-term achievements are at issue. In the former case, school generally refers to years of schooling completed; in the latter, it usually refers to such considerations as contextual characteristics and educational resources treated as properties of the school itself or as teacher influence and track placement treated as elements of individual experience entailed in school attendance. In short, despite variations in the question asked and in the particular components of school production and status attainment formulations, most such studies in fact address very much the same question. They explain variation in individual attainment but with somewhat different constellations of independent variables. They do not, and cannot, respond to questions about the nature of productive processes simply because the complex network of associations among productive conditions is not examined. To know what set of conditions, taken one at a time or all together, influences the learning of individuals is not to know how such conditions are organized to form a productive technology.

We contend in this book that school production research should be concerned both with the social organization of production and with the determination of educational outcomes. Recently, however, two arguments have been expounded that question the soundness of this proposition. The first maintains that it is unnecessary to investigate the productive processes of school organization because there is limited variation among the forms of schooling and because the significant factor explaining individual achievement is whether or not children attend school, not the qualities of the school they attend. The second maintains that the impact of school on students through its organizational activities is a distinctly secondary question. The fundamental impact of schooling, by contrast, is institutional and comes through the symbolic identities it confers, identities that have currency in various sectors of the educational system as well as in the noneducational sectors (like the economy and the family) of society. In neither case is the matter of how schools work and how they produce of much salience.

In her book on summer learning, Heyns (1978) argues that the only way to identify what the school produces is to compare what children learn when enrolled and not enrolled. She treats two status attainment processes, one taking place while school is in session, the other while it is closed for the summer when the influences of family and peers increase in strength and those of the school decline. While treating school effects as status attainments, she also undertakes a critique of formulations that make school quality the cornerstone of school production research. Here we find Heyns citing Hauser's (1969) well-known critique of school production research. "While carefully documenting the fact that differences between high schools explained at best a very small portion of the variance in achievement, course marks, and aspirations, Hauser . . . also provided a cogent and compelling critique of studies that focused on school quality. Schooling, Hauser . . . asserts, 'is differentiated temporally, not territorially . . . ' and 'being in school rather than out of school is far more important than the school one attends' " (Heyns 1978, p. 60; Hauser 1969, pp. 589–90). Support for this contention comes from evidence of the modest impact of school quality and resources on achievement based on such comparisons among schools as the Coleman report. That support is persuasive, however, only if the substantial within-school events are attributed to processes of individual status attainment and not to productive events occurring internal to schools, say, in classrooms. In short, the Heyns-Hauser position resolves the confusion between school production and status attainment models by rendering the former irrelevant. For example: "The effects of schooling are to be understood *by contrasting patterns of cognitive growth* when schools are open to those that prevail when schools are closed during the summer" (Heyns 1978, p. 9; our italics), not by contrasting school properties and operations. In short, school influences in the school production sense are not relevant; schooling effects are processes of status attainment, in the short run, such as achievement, or patterns of cognitive growth.

It is important to appreciate how decisively "school" has been conceptually ruled out of this formulation and replaced by schooling as status attainment. Schooling, according to Heyns, "is unobserved; education is the hypothetical construct accounting for the achievement processes depicted. Yet the goal is a precise quantitative estimate of the additive and interactive effects of schooling over time" (1978, p. 72). One wonders, then, just what it is about schooling, that prima facie might be connected to the nature of schools, that affects achievement; or, in other words, why the status attainment process might be different when school is open from when it is closed. Presumably there is something school-like going on that makes Heyns want to call the attainment process occurring within schools schooling rather than something else; yet the earlier experience with the models of school differences and effects seems to make the examination of school characteristics unpromising. Heyns observes, then, that "attending school . . . increases the achievement for all children, but also reduces the impact of parental status on outcomes to a significant degree" (1978, p. 77). These effects of attending school are equivalent to treating a set of repeated observations as if they were a time series. "The relationship between posttest and pretest would be assumed to depend on socioeconomic status, race, prior achievement, and whether or not schools were in session. *Schooling would then assume the status of a seasonal adjustment*" (p. 77; our italics).

This formulation drains from schooling all elements of school that originate in school properties. Schooling effects refer to a "seasonal adjustment" of the effects of socioeconomic status, race, and prior achievement on current achievement. But that does not seem to be quite the case because Heyns later brings in concepts that sound remarkably like school properties. Thus: "*Schooling* augments achievement in a relatively uniform manner, by exposing all children to a *common academic environment*, irrespective of differences in their backgrounds" (p. 89; our italics). School, then, at least in the form of a "common academic environment," whose commonness strikes us as dubious, has reentered through the back door; such an environment is not defended in this argument as an element in status attainment processes. It remains conceptually undeveloped and empirically undescribed, its properties and operation unexamined.

Heyns has fashioned a persuasive explication of the status attainment perspective as well as an empirical demonstration showing how schooling influences achievement while school is open and how it yields in its influence to the family when it is closed over the summer. At the same time, we believe, the analysis of school organization and operation (the baby) has been thrown out with the inadequacies—empirical, methodological, and conceptual—of school production research (the bathwater). Moreover, the approach is part of a general trend in status attainment research to present the contextual effects of classes, curricula, school, district, and macropolitical conditions as "somehow inferior in methodological status to the individual effects [of student properties]" (Meyer 1980, p. 20). Meyer continues: "Many researchers are uncomfortable with higher level, direct contextual effects on student outcomes . . . They suppose that if higher level effects occur, they should be rendered indirect by discovering what lower level and individual variables mediate them" (Meyer 1980, p. 21; see also Bidwell and Kasarda 1980).

While Meyer (1977) criticizes the reduction of the school production question to one of individual status attainment, he in turn dissolves school production in a different way and in a different direction by invoking the concept of organizational charter and by treating educational effects as symbolic designations of an institutional order. Like Heyns, Meyer takes the weak and inconclusive findings of school production research to indicate that the effectiveness of schools lies not in the impact of their internal workings on the socialization of individuals, but in something else. In addition, his position rests on the notion that because schools are loosely structured and their activities intermittently controlled (Bidwell 1965; Weick 1976) their claim to competence as agencies of socialization should not be taken too seriously.

But what is the something else? According to Meyer, the efficacy of schools lies in their charter, the "features [of an organization] which lie largely *outside its own structure* and which constitute its relation with its social setting. One such feature—perhaps the most important—is the social definition of the products of the organization" (1970, p. 568; our italics). For example, among the most important things that schools produce are alumni, categories of persons subject to social definitions of varying quality which have meaning in the various places that alumni go. He presents here a view of school outcomes not as products of the school's operations but of its institutionalized definition (vocational school, elite college preparatory school, small sectarian college, etc.). These definitions serve as a circulating medium that allows exchanges to take place through accepted definitions of what has value among different parts of a society or other social systems (Green 1980). Such a medium makes more likely, for example, the exchange of a technical school diploma for a job in a trade than for a place in the freshman class of an elite college, independently of how bright the diploma holder is; the exchange of a master's rather than a bachelor's degree for a teaching post, independently of the competence acquired through training.

The key to this process of social definition lies in the institutional, not the productive, functions of the school, in broad aspects of social definition that span major sectors of society. Meyer argues that "modern educational systems involve large-scale public classification systems, defining new roles and statuses for both elites and members. These classifications are new constructions in that the newly defined persons are expected (and entitled) to behave, and be treated by others, in new ways. Not only new types of persons but also new competencies are authoritatively created. Such legitimating effects of education transcend the effects education may have on individuals being processed by the schools. The former effects transform the behavior of people in society quite independent of their own educational experience" (1977, p. 56; Meyer 1980).

While there is much to commend in Meyer's identifying the long-neglected treatment of the institutional functions of education, his subordination of socialization functions appears premature in the absence of adequate treatment of educational production inside schools and its effects. Moreover, while the case for loose structure (or coupling) and intermittent control over instruction is persuasive when viewed from school and district perspectives (Cohen et al. 1976), the closeness of instructional monitoring of classes and instructional groups has yet to be considered. In effect, the weakness of centralized regulation and evaluation of instruction does not mean that these activities fail to be performed at lower levels. Accordingly, in the absence of evidence, this weakness cannot be taken to mean that schools do not take the impact of their instructional efforts seriously.

Heyns, by reducing school production into individual status attainment, and Meyer, by rendering it as an epiphenomenon of broader institutional events, both abandon the question of how schools work. The unpromising results of most studies of school level effects make that a tempting solution. Nevertheless, there remains the still open course of treating organizational variation within schools, the course taken in this book. It will be one burden of our study to show that a more appropriate response to the inadequacies of earlier school production research would have been to formulate school production more adequately, not to jettison the whole enterprise. There is now massive documentation for the proposition that schooling contributes to the processes of status transmission and attainment. The jury is still out, however, on what it is about schools that constitutes schooling and that contributes to attainment.

A recrudescent interest in schooling from a modified production function perspective has shown two major trends: first, a positive interest in classroom organization rather than in the schools in the belief that educational effects are more likely to be observed if measured close to where their actual work gets done; and second, a positive interest in identifying the components of educational technology. Interestingly, economists have directed their attention to the classroom: most particularly, Murnane (1975) to teacher characteristics; Summers (1979; Summers and Wolfe 1974) to matching teachers' and students' characteristics in the same class and identifying reading programs and the classroom organization of reading instruction; Thomas (1977) to patterns of resource allocation—particularly time allocation—within classrooms; and Brown and Saks (1980) to the notion that a job shop model of classroom production is more appropriate than the factory model implicit in the production function scheme.

The general thrust of this work, in contrast to status attainment approaches, draws attention back to the school, its parts, and its workings to determine the character of school production. It indicates concern with the character of educational technology, with what it is about schools (and their parts) of an organizational and a technological nature that enables them to produce learning.

There is an important distinction to be made between studies of production and studies of attainment even though the two come close to converging at certain points. In our view, attempts to account for variations in the life chances of individuals on the basis of their background and experiences are studies of status attainment. It does not matter whether we look at learning gains occurring over a two week period generated by some curricular program, or to variations in earnings at age sixty attributable to socioeconomic background and amount of schooling. Whatever we take to be relevant terms on the right side of the equation—individual socioeconomic status, the influence of significant others, class and school characteristics, job history, and the like— if the left side of the equation refers to some form of individual achievement, we are talking generically about status attainment.

However, individual status attainment is only one kind of educational outcome, by definition restricted to the individual level. Outcomes need not be so limited; indeed, they can be identified at the classroom, school, and district levels. And as we explain in later chapters of this book, a variety of outcomes including those appearing in classes, schools, and districts, in addition to individual attainments, should be included in the investigation of educational production and its effects. .

By contrast, production studies are something else: they do not try to account only for attainments, whether individual or collective, but in addition identify the nature of and variation in the productive process. They are concerned with social organization and technology. For example, when we speak of production in classrooms, we refer to instructional arrangements and activities. The investigation of instruction, as many observers have incorrectly implied, does not pertain directly to learning (or to other attainments). A theory of learning has only limited relevance to the analysis of educational production because it pertains to what happens in children's heads and not to what happens in parts of schools. Needed, then, is a formulation of how instruction is organized in classrooms and in groups located inside them. At all levels of school systems, production entails the mobilization and allocation of resources and the design of appropriate forms of social organization to produce outcomes. More specifically, in districts and schools, production must be understood as governance and administration; within schools, it consists of class formation, group formation, and instruction.

Given this distinction between school production and status attainment, we must distinguish further between the level of analysis and the substantive concern of the investigator. Take the case of the Coleman report. Coleman and his colleagues (1966) compared schools and determined whether differences between them were responsible for how much students learned. They did not, however, compare the average achievement of schools (as did Brookover et al. 1979), which would have been one way to assess school effects; instead, they assigned the characteristics of schools to each individual student while controlling for certain individual characteristics. In fact, Coleman et al., by our strict definition, investigated status attained (achievement) by individuals. Their substantive interest, however, centered on the characteristics of schools; that is to say, the categories of the independent variables pertained largely to school properties.

If we keep this same *substantive* point in mind, the Hauser-Heyns line of investigation, for example, centered on different independent variables that pertained to aspects of individual careers and life chances; but *methodologically*, just like Coleman et al. (1966), they analyzed data at the individual level. To clarify the general point, we make the following juxtapositions: methodologically, Alexander and McDill (1976), Coleman et al. (1966), Heyns (1978), and Summers (1979) all investigate status attainment because they are concerned with variation in individual status (or achievement) accounted for by variations in individual experiences. Substantively, Alexander and McDill (1976), Bidwell and Kasarda (1975), Brown and Saks (1980), Burkhead, Fox, and Holland (1967), Coleman et al. (1966), and Summers (1979) are all concerned with school production; but methodologically, some pursue it at the individual level and others at higher organizational levels (schools, classes, and districts). Note that we have included two of these studies in both lists to illustrate the difference between substance and methodology.

We are trying to press the case here that understanding educational production depends upon the proper identification of organizational levels; but that is not our only case. Once the levels have been correctly specified, it is still necessary to characterize the nature of resources that come into play at each of them, to describe how they are related to each other to form coherent productive activities, and to establish how these activities yield their respective outcomes. There is no reason to assume that simply adding individual characteristics and experiences through statistical procedures to create class, school, and district aggregations will provide conceptually adequate representations of how school production works.

Over the preceding pages, we have tried to draw attention to what we believe are some important distinctions for understanding how schools work. Primary among them is the distinction between production and its effects. To identify the organization of production is one thing; to identify the determinants of individual achievements quite another. The latter subsumes the investigation of status attainment and of human capital from both short- and long-run perspectives and is part of the wider consideration of status transmission and of individual social mobility. The former refers to the fundamental Marxian concept, stripped of its ideological baggage, of the "social relations of production," of how people are organized in their productive pursuits to create values. To understand how schools work and what their effects are we need to formulate how these distinct ideas—production and attainment—can be brought together. Yet, they must not be confused with each other; the analytical distinction between them must be preserved while the empirical connections between them are established. Production in schools, classrooms, and instructional groups consists of the attempts by administrators and teachers to organize time, resources, and aggregations of children into an instructional program; it is not the sum of the experiences of individual children. Those experiences obviously influence individual learning, but school production pertains to the arrangement and organization of activities that shape those experiences. Through an indirect route, school production does yield individual attainments, but along with a variety of other outcomes not all of which can be properly expressed at the individual level.

Psychological and Instructional Approaches

Until recently, except for a brief period of intensive collaboration at the beginning of the century, psychologists and educational researchers have followed different pursuits. According to Glaser (1978), while psychologists turned to the laboratory to pursue research guided primarily by theoretical concerns, educational researchers, even though guided by psychological premises and methodologies, explored practical issues of teaching, curriculum, and testing.

The search by educational researchers during the first half of this century for conditions influencing student learning was extensive and included such variables as ability grouping, student involvement, teacher characteristics, amount of instruction, instructional methods, and class size. More impressive than the volume of this research, however, was its repeated failure to document expected relations. Stephens, following a systematic review of this literature, concluded that "the constancy of the school's accomplishments is one of those things that everybody knows. It is part of the folklore that, in educational investigations, one method turns out to be as good as another and that promising innovations produce about as much as the procedures they supplant, but no more" (1967, pp. 9–10).

The response of educational researchers to the indictments of inconclusiveness, instability, and inconsistency was not to give up the enterprise of studying classroom instruction but rather to turn to alternative methodologies, in particular to the observation of teachers' interaction with their students (Bellack et al. 1966; Flanders 1965; Medley and Mitzel 1958, Meux and Smith 1964). And while the study of instruction has evolved into a vast and amorphous enterprise, we nevertheless believe that only a very small number of different schemes have become elaborated over time. We have identified two of them: one concerned with the effects of teaching on learning (teacher effectiveness), and a second with the effects of time allocations on learning (instructional time). We consider these bodies of research in the subsequent sections of this chapter; by contrast, because of their simplistic methodologies and formulations that carry us conceptually such little distance, we do not consider traditional educational studies.

In recent years, psychologists have again turned their attention to problems that bear on school learning. The decade of the seventies spawned a vast literature on mental processes in response to textual material and other verbal stimuli (e.g., Anderson et al. 1977; Ausubel, Novak, and Hanesian 1978; Kintsch 1974; Rothkopf 1970) and on individual learning in response to specially designed curricular sequences (e.g., Greeno 1978; Lesgold and Curtis 1981; Resnick 1976; Suppes and Morningstar 1972).

Work in cognitive psychology that employs brief textual passages, real and contrived, with individual readers in nonclassroom settings has limited relevance to understanding classroom instruction and learning, however informative such research might be for exploring the dimensions of the mind. Further, the investigation of individual learning from specially developed curricula, even those used in classroom settings, is of limited value in understanding the productive work of schools because such curricula frequently represent isolated experimental intrusions into the ordinary activities of the school or substitutes for them, and for those reasons they obscure its ordinary workings. Formulations of mental functioning (cognition) deal with the responses of the mind to external stimulation but cannot (nor are they intended to) deal with how the stimuli get there in the first place or with how they are organized in the course of the school's operations and through teaching activities. These last two questions are central to the investigation of instruction, but they cannot be answered when the stimuli are designed and presented by a psychologist in the course of investigating individual mental functioning and learning. We turn, then, to the recent educational research on classroom instruction in order to delineate existing methodologies and formulations.

Teacher Effectiveness

Work on the impact of teaching on learning has been dominated by the so-called process-product approach to teacher effectiveness, an approach associated with Brophy and Evertson (1974), Dunkin and Biddle (1974), Gage (1964, 1972, 1978), and Rosenshine (1971) as well as others. The hallmark of the process-product approach is the analysis of teaching into such elements as activities and goals. With respect to activities, for example, Gage indicates that teaching can be analyzed into explaining, demonstrating, guiding, order maintaining, housekeeping, record keeping, assignment making, curriculum planning, testing, "and many other kinds of activities. If everything a teacher does qua teacher is teaching, then teaching consists of many kinds of activity" (1972, p. 275). Indeed, teaching has been analyzed into these elements, but to what analytical purpose? How long does the list run, and what are the connections among its items?

With such an open-ended compilation of elements, process-product research is distinguished, not surprisingly, by being short on formulation and conceptual argumentation and long on data gathering; accordingly, the nature of the formulation only becomes discernible by inference from descriptions of what investigators working in this tradition do. In its elementary form, the scheme makes provision for two categories of entities: "*Process variables* concern the actual activities of classroom teaching—what teachers and pupils *do* in the classroom" (Dunkin and Biddle 1974, p. 44). "*Product variables* concern the outcomes of teaching—those changes that come about in pupils as a result of their involvement in classroom activities with teachers and other pupils" (Dunkin and Biddle 1974, p. 46).

The scheme also appears to include in somewhat more elaborate form teacher background and such elements of context as pupil, classroom, and community characteristics.

While including two categories of phenomena and exploring how they are related, this scheme does not say anything about what specific things should go into them. While any kind of teacher activity might be related to any kind of outcome, the approach provides no guidance for arguing substantively from teacher behavior to pupil outcome or for believing why any particular variable should be related to another. Accordingly, few studies tie together context, teacher characteristics, process, and product or explain why certain conditions are included while others are left out.

The effect of this approach to research on teaching effectiveness is that no limits (defined by conceptual principles of relevance) are set upon the range of teaching activities worth examining. We find, for example, a review of process-product research that lists forty-one aspects of teacher conduct, each represented by several studies, containing several hundred zero-order correlations (Rosenshine 1971). Similarly, Brophy and Evertson (1974) have examined relations between several hundred teaching variables and five measures of outcome. Stallings's (1975) work is similar in nature.

It is no surprise that the arid empiricism of process-product research is plagued with unstable findings and few robust empirical generalizations. The studies prove to be largely uninterpretable because they lack substantive formulation about what classroom instruction is and how it works, about what the phenomenon of classroom teaching is that confers pattern and coherence on its elements. The studies can only be interpreted on an ad hoc basis, finding by finding, a direct result of the elements of teaching having been identified only on the basis of plausibility and of the use of similar variables in the past. And while the annals of process-product research undoubtedly contain important findings, the formulation itself is incapable of identifying which among the multitude they are or why they are important.

It would be wrong to suggest that process-product research totally ignores questions of context; Dunkin and Biddle include such considerations in a graphic representation of their model (1974, p. 38) but not in a way that indicates a concern with conditional relations. Doyle (1978) also discusses contextual (i.e., ecological) conditions, but they dissolve into students' perceptions and ways of coping with aspects of the class environment and thus lose their contextual status. Brophy and Evertson (1974) interpret their findings separately in high and low socioeconomic status schools as well as for morning and afternoon hours of the day, but they provide no persuasive rationale for including these particular conditions as indicated by their application of them across the board to hundreds of separate correlations. We shall return to the elaborations of the process-product scheme shortly, for the introduction of conditional and intervening variables has been one of the ways by which the primitive form of the scheme has become developed.

While the expression "process-product" has gained a rather clear contemporary reference (Doyle 1978), research of the same kind, examining the effects of teaching on learning, has a long history, much of which has a clear conceptual and substantive base. Flanders's (1965) work, for example, grows out of a tradition extending back to the pioneering social-psychological studies of Lewin, Lippitt, and White (1939), and is premised on the idea that teaching should be understood as social interaction that varies along a dimension of directiveness. Direct teaching methods, he argues, create dependency among students and for that reason are inimical to the growth of initiative, independence, and curiosity, which are believed to have salutary influences upon achievement. In a conceptually similar but substantively distinct formulation, Meux and Smith (1964) concern themselves with teaching as verbal behavior and discourse which carries meaning through the logical and intellectual operations of explaining, describing, defining, classifying, comparing, and the like, that get communicated to students and then transformed into the same operational skills. Bellack and his colleagues (1966) follow Meux and Smith in a somewhat different direction, examining teaching as a language game whose grammar is tied to the activities of classroom instruction: soliciting verbal contributions and activities from students, responding to them, structuring their activities, and reacting to what they do and say.

While this is far from an exhaustive summary of approaches to teaching, we find here, in contrast to the process-product scheme, substantive statements about what teaching is. These statements define what is important to observe about teaching and provide guiding principles that characterize it. Whether one agrees with the formulation and whether it stands up to empirical scrutiny are beside the point, which is that the analysis of educational production at whatever level must contain a substantive formulation that identifies the central activities of teaching and indicates how they are organized, how they affect learning, and under what conditions.

Among the most patent inadequacies of the process-product scheme is its failure to consider children, their characteristics and activities, as the transformers of instruction into outcomes. However, we find several investigators addressing precisely that flaw. For example, Rothkopf's work on mathemagenic activities identifies those mental activities that intervene between nominal stimuli (such as teachers' instruction) and outcomes, and are presumed to result from effective stimuli. Acts that transform nominal into effective stimuli "have been called set, attention, orienting reflex, information processing, cognition, rehearsal, and so on. All of these acts fall within the broad boundaries of the term *mathemagenic* activities" (1970, p. 326). Walberg (1977), by contrast, suggests that the perceptions of students should be treated as intervening events between learning environments and achievement. While Walberg emphasizes conscious and overt assessments and descriptions of instructional or classroom influences in contrast to the "invisible" workings of Rothkopf's mathemagenic activities and in contrast to Anderson and his colleagues' (1977) schemata, the logic of the two positions is precisely the same: namely, events intervening between the influence and the outcome must be examined, events internal to the students themselves. And while Rothkopf and Anderson et al. (1977) are not explicitly interested in classroom instruction (but rather in instruction as it pertains to textual material), Walberg and his colleagues (1974) develop a warehouse inventory of classroom characteristics related to instruction (the learning environment inventory—fifteen dimensions, seven items per dimension) closely resembling the process-product approach.

Including intervening events in the process-product formulation does more than specify some plausible mechanisms that transform instruction into learning outcomes; it implicitly acknowledges that many events occur in classrooms at the same time. By examining only one element of teaching at a time, the process-product formulation in effect explodes classroom instruction into fragments of zero-order relations. Even the most casual observations of classrooms indicate a certain patterning of teacher and student conduct, a certain coherence even when things appear disorganized. Yet how is it possible to portray dominant social and instructional patterns without a conceptual apparatus for determining relations *among* instructional conditions as well as relations between those conditions, taken one at a time, and some measure of learning outcome? It is not possible.

While some investigators have argued for including one or another second instructional condition into zero-order relations (Rothkopf and Walberg being apposite examples), Cronbach and Snow have developed a systematic methodological approach to treating instruction-outcome relations as conditional. In what they call aptitude-treatment-interaction, "The scientific problem is to locate interactions of individual differences among learners with instructional treatments" (1977, p. 2). The idea is that methods of instruction have different outcomes depending upon the individual differences of students, in particular, their aptitudes, where aptitude is "any characteristic of a person that forecasts his probability of success under a given treatment" (p. 6).

Aptitude-treatment-interaction (ATI) applied to the area of instruction is in part an attempt to find coherence in an area of inquiry characterized by inconsistency. The thought is that the difficulty of generalizing from a large store of amorphous empirical findings could be reduced if some relations were shown to be conditional but nonetheless patterned. Conditional analysis, however, did not remedy the situation, as Cronbach notes with some pessimism: "An ATI result can be taken as a general conclusion only if it is not in turn moderated by further variables . . . Once we attend to interactions, we enter a hall of mirrors that extends to infinity" (1975, p. 119).

There is probably no wholly adequate solution to the problem of infinite regress. But short of that, there are some remedies if the ailment is correctly diagnosed and if the diagnosis is not made prematurely. Cronbach and Snow perform their conditional analyses on a vast array of empirical relations reported in the literature on instruction. But as they observe, the treatment side of these relations remains largely uncodified. "One can imagine," they note, "five, ten, or even a hundred alternative treatments" (1977, p. 165), "but no one has yet sought to organize these into some hierarchical or other taxonomic structure" (p. 167).

Cronbach and Snow, however, do not themselves undertake a codification of instruction or even attempt a conceptual analysis of the concept "treatment." They reanalyze the literature as it lies, and much of that literature is of the process-product variety: plausible treatments selected ad hoc, one at a time, and without cumulative coherence study to study. Why, then, should one expect conditional analysis to draw disparate and inconsistent findings together when the original main effects were not derived from a clear conception of what instruction entails and how it might work? Conditional analysis would seem to be a more useful strategy for pursuing a clearly formulated argument beyond its initial test and less well suited for reaching into a grab bag of unstable zero-order relations.

Strategic questions aside, the approach seems unnecessarily restrictive on substantive grounds as well. In our view, making individual aptitudes the only type of condition to intervene between treatment and outcome ignores matters of instructional context, situation, and organization which can be just as important as aptitudes in explaining variations in learning. That is, instructional treatments may work better in one kind of classroom setting than in another independently of individual differences in aptitude; or better still, in combination with such differences. The ATI formulation, despite its important methodological contributions, adds little of a substantive nature to the analysis of instruction and its organization. Nevertheless, it strongly builds the ideas of conditionality and simultaneity into the analysis of instruction even though only two elements at a time are treated simultaneously and conditionally. Two, of course, are better than one.

In Bennett's work (1976; Bennett and Jordan 1975) on formal and informal classrooms and their effects upon learning, we find serious interest in the simultaneity of instructional conditions and events. His problem was the multidimensional characterization of classrooms which required an appropriate selection of class properties as well as a means of combining them. He struck upon a statistical solution for combining activities (cluster analysis) which, however, in the nature of the case, makes it impossible for any of the elements within the cluster to serve as conditions for each other. Statistical procedures of this kind are vulnerable to the kind of difficulty that Bennett in fact experienced: that the two extremes of the ostensible continuum distinguishing formal and informal classrooms are not separated by a clear set of intermediate positions; the items making up the continuum, in other words, do not form a scale. Whatever the flaws in the statistical procedure, this work makes a clear contribution to measuring the multidimensional (and simultaneous) nature of instructional activities. Moreover, he treats formal, informal, and intermediate types of classes conditionally in some parts of the work by varying the relation between class types and learning under varying contextual conditions, in particular, whether or not the school prepares its students for the eleven plus examinations.

All in all, Bennett's work advances considerably beyond the process-product approach, which makes no explicit provision for the multiplicity of things occurring at the same time in classrooms. It contrasts favorably with other attempts to codify the large set of zero-order associations between teaching conditions and learning. For example, the recently proposed model of "direct instruction" (Rosenshine 1979), which in substance resembles Bennett's view of formal teaching, serves only to specify a set of conditions such as immediate and academically oriented feedback, teacher control of instructional goals, structured materials, questions asked at a low cognitive level, and the like, that seem to enhance learning. This model, however, is not a formulation of instruction, because it fails to specify how the instructional conditions are connected to each other and to prior conditions. It is simply another—but shorter—list.

While only the most exceptional of teacher effectiveness studies treat relations among the elements of instruction, virtually none identifies a connection between the activities of teachers and the characteristics of the setting in which teaching takes place—the classroom. This means that the only representation of the classroom is the conduct of teachers; it does not appear as an element of school organization. Such considerations, for example, as the composition of children's characteristics and the appropriateness of learning materials for the class, conditions that constrain the instructional efforts of teachers, do not form part of the picture. In the perspective of teacher effectiveness research, teaching hangs suspended in the middle of the air, undisturbed by the organization in which it takes place, by the clients, and by the educational resources intended to produce learning.

Instructional Time

From the work of Carroll (1963), a distinct and parallel line of conceptualization and investigation has developed containing a clear formulation of educational effects. In his model of school learning, which is not that at all but rather a model of individual learning, Carroll argues that time spent by children in learning activities is a key determinant of how much they learn; and as we shall see, his concern with time has had a perduring influence on the study of educational effects at the classroom and individual levels. Carroll identifies the determinants of aptitude (that is, time needed for learning): the ability to understand instruction, and the quality of instruction (as well as other personal characteristics). He also identifies the determinants of time spent in learning: time made available and perseverance. Among the most important attributes of this formulation, in contrast to the process-product scheme, is its identification of a small number of centrally important conceptual elements. It has a coherent conceptualization.

Carroll's model, however, virtually ignores the nature of instruction. His comments on "quality of instruction" go very little beyond assertions that instruction should be appropriate: "The learner must be put into adequate sensory contact with the material . . . Aspects of the learning task must be presented in such an order and with such detail that . . . every step of the learning is adequately prepared for . . . The instruction must be adapted for the special needs and characteristics of the learner"

(1963, p. 726). The difficulty with these contentions is first their lack of specificity, and second their sole concern with the learner but not with the elements of instruction. Yet, over time, we find work influenced by Carroll filling out and giving meaning to the vast and nearly empty category of instruction that his model provides while at the same time preserving the central place reserved for time. Later work, moreover, has elaborated the concept of time.

Note that Carroll's formulation has virtually nothing to say about teaching, instruction, classrooms, and schools. It is a model of school learning only insofar as the learning in question takes place in schools; but the schooling components of the model are left unconceptualized. As we indicated above, it is a model of individual learning, the unidentified school and classroom components of which are included in the concept "quality of instruction."

Among the most important elaborations of Carroll's scheme is Bloom's presentation of mastery learning. Unlike those working in the process-product tradition, Bloom (1968, 1976) begins with a real, fundamental, and problematic classroom issue: how can teachers deal with variation in children's aptitudes in classrooms. (Note that Bloom is especially concerned with showing how those variations in aptitude can be translated into roughly equal and high levels of mastery rather than into patterns of direct association between aptitude and achievement. We are not concerned here with that programmatic aspect of his work.) From the standpoint of conceptualizing instruction, Bloom's work adds substance to Carroll's nearly empty category, "quality of instruction." Bloom contends that individual learning proceeds well when children have mastered the prerequisites for what they are about to learn next. Accordingly, the mastery learning scheme puts special emphasis on the proper utilization of time in the classroom to establish among the slower achievers the prerequisites for mastering the next skills. Hence, through carefully sequenced instruction, formative testing, appropriate feedback, and a variety of remedial activities—all to be understood as elements of instruction—time needed to learn, particularly among slower students, is expected to decrease over time.

Bloom does not claim to have developed a general scheme for the analysis of classroom instruction, but rather to have modified an existing model and applied it in programmatic terms to remedy an unfortunate state of affairs in classroom teaching. The conceptual part puts special stress on the temporal dimension of instruction: that time spent on remediation for those who need it will provide the prerequisites for subsequent learning, and that the time needed for remediation will decrease over time with the result that less time is then required by slower students to master material to a given standard on a par with those who master the material more quickly.

We find a more highly formalized conception of instruction based upon both Carroll and Bloom in Harnischfeger and Wiley (1976, 1978), whose work draws as well from the production function tradition. The Harnischfeger-Wiley work on instruction begins with an attempt to show that the amount of schooling children receive rather than its quality explains their learning (Wiley 1973; Wiley and Harnischfeger 1974). This early work speaks directly to purported inadequacies of school effects studies, Coleman's in particular, and claims, though not without dissent (Karweit 1976), that the amount of time children spend in school exposed to the educational influences that schools make available explains a substantial portion of their achievement.

True to its origins in Carroll's model, the Harnischfeger-Wiley work proceeds to the individual level, but also considers the classroom. A formulation that begins with such time elements as length of school year, of school day, and of daily attendance—categories of districts and schools—becomes extended to the allocation of time in classrooms and to the time children spend actively engaged in curricular pursuits. On the classroom side, the model specifies different kinds of organizational formats (whole class, grouped, and individual seatwork arrangements) as well as the degree to which teachers supervise class activities. Unlike the elaborated forms of the process-product formulation and the aptitude-treatment-interaction scheme which regard psychological processes as mediating between teaching and learning, Harnischfeger and Wiley consider the active working time of children to be the major mediator.

This formulation, which shows evidence of considerable care taken in the identification of instructional considerations, nevertheless raises unanswered questions about the connection between instruction and learning. Harnischfeger and Wiley (1976, pp. 28–29) present a conceptual analysis of how teachers allocate their class time (to different curricular activities, to class management, to supervision) along with a separate but related analysis of how teacher time and activity allocations manifest themselves in the experience of individual students (how much each student spends in whole class instruction, in supervised group instruction, in unsupervised individual seatwork, and so on). At first glance, it appears that they are about to formulate the connection between the classroom (and teacher) level and the level of individual children as a way of understanding instruction. But this turns out not to be the case.

Despite the fact that Harnischfeger and Wiley move some considerable distance beyond Carroll in developing a model of school learning by infusing content into Carroll's nearly void category of "quality of instruction," their concern for instruction in reality dissolves into an explanation of individual learning as it occurs in schools. We discover this in their analysis of three instructional settings: total class, subgroup, and seatwork, all treated as both conceptually and empirically independent. If the conditions fostering individual learning are at issue and if, as Harnischfeger and Wiley believe to be the case, different kinds of classroom arrangements affect learning to different degrees, it is possible to assess the instructional experience of each child by determining and adding the amount of time spent in each arrangement. However, if the organization of classroom instruction is at issue, then total class, subgroup, and seatwork instruction are not empirically independent and cannot be added up. Whole class instruction precludes the other two. Subgroup instruction usually takes place only when the teacher assigns unsupervised seatwork to those children who are not immediately involved with the teacher in the subgroup.

In effect, the analysis of classroom organization presents a different problem of formulation from the analysis of individual experiences that eventuate in learning. And while Harnischfeger and Wiley begin with a suggestive analysis of how instruction looks from the teachers' and the students' side, the two lines of analysis and the formulation of their connection are not pursued. What remains is a usefully elaborated formulation of the instructional experiences of individual children that contribute to their school learning, but not a formulation of classroom instruction. We must be careful to observe, moreover, that Harnischfeger and Wiley do not claim to be interested in classroom instruction, just in learning. While their work starts off in the direction of joining the issue between the two different phenomena, it settles in the end for what it promised to do.

By this time, we should recognize a familiar friend: a model of status attainment that grew, not out of research on status attainment, but from a critique of school effects research and from a model of individual learning based upon time spent engaged in learning activities. The status to be attained, of course, is the level of short-term individual achievement in some specified curricular activity. While this scheme identifies elements of instruction, it does not represent a formulation of instruction; for while it substantively fleshes out the original Carroll model with respect to the meaning of instruction, the new terms introduced—grouping, supervision, materials, curriculum area, explanation, task organization, and the like—are not further analyzed, nor are they treated at any other but the individual level. The model says that if we know, for example, how much time a particular child has spent doing math, using a given set of materials, on a task that is explained more or less clearly, in one or another kind of class, under more or less close supervision, we can expect that child to have learned so much.

As we indicated earlier, this kind of proposition, even if it accounts for variation in individual learning, tells us nothing about the organization of instruction because it pertains only to the sum of individual experiences. Understanding instruction requires that we know what aspects of grouping, supervision, materials, curriculum, and the like, are important, and that we know how these elements work in combination as phenomena of the classroom, not as aspects of individual students' experience.

Harnischfeger and Wiley's scheme implies that certain elements of classroom organization should be understood quantitatively as represented by time; that is, children learn more in a given content area depending on the amount of time they spend, say, in grouped or whole class instruction under varying degrees of supervision. This scheme, however, does not address the qualitative aspects of classroom organization and instruction—for example, what kinds of groups, what kinds of supervision, and so on. Other elements of instruction, such as the nature of instructional materials, receive no serious conceptual development; and although the frequency with which materials are used is undoubtedly an important matter, surely the qualitative properties of materials also deserve attention.

Phase III of the Beginning Teacher Evaluation Study (Fisher et al. 1978) addresses some of these issues. The BTES formulation also belongs in the school effects–status attainment category, concerned with the explanation of individual learning. On the surface, it employs a now familiar format: achievement, children's learning activities, their aptitudes, and elements of the classroom instructional environment, with time being the critical element of learning activities. Time, however, undergoes some conceptual elaboration. The BTES scheme retains the familiar dimensions of time available and time spent actively engaged. It takes cognizance of the fact that learning depends not only on time engaged in a task but also on the difficulty of the task. Accordingly: "Time spent by a student engaged in a task on which few errors are produced, and where the task is directly relevant to an academic outcome, constitutes a measure of student classroom learning behavior" (1978, p. 2-4).

The notion of task difficulty, included within the four-part concept of "academic learning time" (allocated time, engaged time, error rate, and relevance to a content domain, p. 2-4), gives the BTES model its particular stamp. "When a student works on a specific task, there is an interaction between the characteristics of the task and the current ability of the student to complete the task. A given student will learn more from some tasks than from others. Hence there are degrees of appropriateness among tasks which affect student learning. For a given student, periods of time spent on tasks differing in this kind of appropriateness will be quite different in quality and will affect the amount the student learns" (p. 2-5). Error rate, treated as an intervening variable with respect to instructional activities and classroom context, is a concept designed to capture this interactive property of aptitude and task difficulty.

We consider the development of academic learning time with its error rate component to be important because it introduces qualitative properties of learning activities (task difficulty) into arguments hitherto restricted to their quantitative aspects (amount of time). More important, the error rate concept provides at least one way of understanding how aptitude-treatment-interaction relations work. According to the latter scheme, treatments may have different effects on learning depending on variations in aptitude. One reason for this conditionality may be that one of the treatments is well suited to high aptitude children and poorly suited to low aptitude children. By this reasoning, a qualitative aspect of instruction (for example, task difficulty) is identified that can interpret how a conditional relation works by specifying the mechanism, although BTES does not develop this argument.

The BTES study also concerns itself with the nature of the instructional environment and turns at least in part to the process-product scheme (or rather to its warehouse inventory) for its qualitative characterizations. There are two major components to the instructional environment: one pertaining to instructional activities, the other to classroom context. The former refers to such activities as presenting and explaining academic information, monitoring the performance of children, and providing feedback, all measured by the proportion of instructional time spent in the subject area. The latter refers to global assessments of climate, such as "enthusiasm, warmth, competitiveness, cooperation, and task orientation" (p. 2-11). These elements are then put together by using the format of conditional analysis. Thus, for example, "Differences in environmental variables may mediate the relationship between teacher process variables and facets of academic learning time" (p. 2-11). Note also the important substantive difference between this statement and the Cronbach-Snow position: in BTES, organizational properties like climate can mediate between teaching activities and an outcome such as academic learning time, while in the Cronbach-Snow formulation only individual aptitudes mediate between treatments and outcomes. By contrast, BTES rules out the instructional importance of aptitudes through covariation, while Cronbach and Snow retain aptitudes to represent key conditions affecting the relation between instructional treatments and outcomes. Neither scheme, however, undertakes to consider a full range of mediating and conditional events, from the characteristics of individuals to elements of social organization, that may influence the way in which learning outcomes are produced.

With this characterization of the BTES formulation, we have shown how a simple time model and a simple model of teacher effectiveness have become refined and elaborated by restricting the number of contributions to learning deemed important, by framing those contributions in coherent, substantive conceptions (though not necessarily complete ones), and by introducing mediating conditions and processes. We arrive, then, at a temporary destination where the two basic classroom instruction models become conjoined in the BTES formulation. The joint product, moreover, represents another expression of the status attainment formulation in which time spent learning and subsequently learning itself are attributed to the experiences of individuals in their encounters with the characteristics of classrooms and teaching activities. Lost in the shuffle is the matter of school production and class organization, for while the process-product formulation is basically formulated at the classroom level, presumably to deal with the nature of teaching, it does not possess a conceptual apparatus that deals with the productive elements of classrooms.

IMPLICATIONS

The Workings of Schools and Their Effects

Our review indicates that the overwhelming interest of most past work is in the effects of schooling and not in how schools work to produce them. This is not surprising when we consider the historical period that generated most of this research, characterized as it was by preoccupation with the equal distribution of the results of educational experience as a right of citizenship. Overarching interests in equality led to investigations of the distribution and correlates of values, not to how they were created in the first place. Studies of status attainment had their own internal logic, bounded at both ends by socioeconomic considerations: Given the socioeconomic background of individuals, how does education contribute to the transmission of initial status within the same generation and into the next? School production studies are more problematic in that they require a conjuring up of independent variables to account for variations in short-run achievement.

We argue that in investigations of both school and classroom instructional effects, plausibility rules the day in the selection of explanatory conditions that singly or in combination are designed to account for the results of schooling. But plausibility simply provides no criterion for distinguishing what is important from what is not. The empirical record is poor; but even more disquieting, little groundwork is laid for developing a formulation that might guide the selection of explanatory considerations and better still determine how they might fit together. With little impetus to think about how work in school systems is organized, without distinctions made between the availability of resources (as influences upon school outcomes) and the use of those resources, and with the widespread use of linear regression techniques that abet the tendency to add up the contributory influences on schooling outcomes rather than think about the variety of alternative ways that such influences might be combined, the matter of how schools work failed to clear the threshold of importance.

As Baron and Bielby observe, there has been a "tendency of analysts to confound two questions: 'How is work organized?' and 'Who gets ahead?' " (1980, p. 738). Especially among studies on the impact of schooling, the first of those questions has hardly been addressed, though with certain notable exceptions. But to our view, a conception of school production is central. For if it can be presented as a coherent formulation, then it is possible to establish connections between what the schools produce and how they produce it in reasonably parsimonious terms.

The Organizational Levels of School Systems

The formulation of production rests upon a satisfactory understanding of how the labor of school systems is divided among its levels. Most research on educational effects, whether of the production, attainment, or instructional variety, focuses on a single level of analysis, usually the individual level. People naturally differ about what is appropriate, and most acknowledge that different problems require different levels of analysis. But while there is no argument against doing what is appropriate, the preoccupation with one level or another obscures the possibility that productive events occur over several levels.

Some investigators are patently aware that the events that constitute schooling occur in different places; that some contributions come from principals, some from teachers, and others from students themselves. To accommodate these differently located influences, everything is expressed at the level of the individual student, with the result that school or class events become dissolved into individual experiences. In the process the character of productive processes taking place in schools and classes—expressed in school and class terms—is lost. Others argue that school organization is loosely coupled so that the connections between levels tend toward randomness. In both ways, we lose our grip on the events that constitute school production and that influence its outcomes.

Our work is based on the general presupposition that when labor is divided, there is a reason for it; and that when people set about accomplishing distinct tasks in different parts of an organization, one should pay attention to what they do and to how the parts fit together. We are building upon the familiar insight of Parsons that organizations have qualitatively distinct levels of a technical, managerial, and institutional kind, each having an agenda of its own to work out and each being tied through interchanges to the adjacent one. Our point is not to affirm the particular utility of his three types but rather to show how the typology itself draws attention to the importance of identifying the special contribution of each level to the organization's total operation. "There has been a tendency," he observed, "to neglect the importance of what in some sense are qualitative breaks in the continuity of the line structure" (1963, p. 59).

A major implication of this perspective is to attend to the particular nature of events that occur at the district, school, class, group, and individual student level of school system organization. By further implication, it means raising the possibility that each level of organization produces its own outcomes, or values, which in turn have meaningful connections to events that occur elsewhere. This view acknowledges that learning is a critically important value of school production, particularly at the level of individual students, but it questions deeply the prevailing assumption that it is necessarily an important outcome at any other level of school system organization. Nevertheless, the productive events and outcomes at these other levels might have a strong impact on learning through a series of hierarchical connections.

3. Levels of School Organization

The central problem in understanding the division of labor in school organization is to identify what the important resources are, where they are located, how they vary, and how they are used. The record of past research on both school effects and classroom instruction tells us that trying to find the determinants of school learning by adding up the effects of numerous plausible conditions leads into an empirical cul de sac. A different strategy needs to be followed, one that involves risks in identifying only a small number of important resources selected on the basis of a conceptual analysis of what we believe to be key elements of school production: certain characteristics of children, the nature of instructional materials, time, and the activities of teachers that govern the use of materials over time.

The record also shows that the attempts to identify effective conditions of schooling have been governed by efforts to specify the one most appropriate level of analysis. But ordinary observation of school systems reveals that educationally important activities occur at all levels, and for this reason we must show what things happen where, and how the resources entailed in school production manifest themselves at different locations—levels—of the organization. And finally, because production consists of activity, it is not the stockpiles of available resources that

43

should primarily concern us, but the uses to which they are actually put.

Although we shall discuss all levels of school system organization in this chapter, we are primarily interested in the workings of classrooms. But what happens there is tied up with events occurring elsewhere in the school system, which is the reason for trying to make sense of the larger picture. Among the class conditions that bear most directly on instructional design, we have not included every plausible aspect, but only a small number of underlying considerations. There are, in our view, just a few key problems and a small number of solutions that teachers use to resolve them. Beyond that, there are numerous variations in style, nuance, tactic, and idiosyncrasy that can all too readily be mistaken for the main story. We attempt here to relate the main story, the central set of considerations that lie at the core of classroom instruction.

EMPIRICAL ANALYSIS

To test the logic of our emerging formulation of classroom instruction, we undertook the secondary analysis of an existing body of data (Barr 1971, 1973–74, 1975). Three characteristics of the evidence proved useful for our purposes. These pertained to the selection of schools and classes, the sampling of individuals, and the assessment of classroom conditions.

Characteristics of the Evidence

In the original data, two schools were studied in each of three districts. The first district (I) was located in a predominantly lower to lower-middle class, largely black urban neighborhood in Chicago; the second (II) in an old suburban, middle to upper-middle class, white neighborhood adjacent to the city limits; and the third (III) in a more recently developed suburban white working to lower-middle class neighborhood. The schools were identified by central office personnel as being representative of other schools in the district and as having principals willing to participate in a research project.

In each school, several classrooms were studied with one exception: in one district I school, only one of the three teachers agreed to participate. But as shown in table 3.1, in all other schools (B–F), at least two classes were studied. The existence of more than one case at a given organizational level—two schools in a district, two classes in a school—allowed us to contrast cases within levels and to identify discontinuities in resource allocation. We could also organize the evidence into subsets corresponding to the individual, instructional group, class, school, and district levels of organization. This reclassification of the evidence permitted us to pursue our interest in higher level organizational influences on lower level phenomena, to conduct analyses across organizational levels, and to treat variations both among organizational properties and among individuals at any given level.

The sample included individual data for a random and numerically substantial proportion of each class so that we could reconstruct the distributional properties of classes and estimate some properties of instructional groups. In the original study, undertaken to test the reliability and validity of a reading readiness instrument, samples of students, stratified on the basis of sex, were randomly selected from each grade cohort. As a consequence, as shown in table 3.1, the proportion of students representing each class differs and ranges from 22 to 50 percent. While an average sampling ratio of about 34 percent with fluctuations above and below is not what one would like to rely on for the rigorous testing of hypotheses (which is not what we are doing), it is respectable for the task we have undertaken: to rethink the way in which school production has been conceptualized. We are not trying to generalize from the empirical evidence, but rather to demonstrate how the formulation applies to the realities of schooling. The fact that the cases were well sampled is extremely important because it allows us to examine how the distributive properties of classes influence the establishment of instructional arrangements.

Finally, the evidence proved valuable because it included indices of important class resources—estimates of the aptitude and learning of children, descriptions of the instructional materials and their use, records of daily time schedules, and indices of teaching experience (see table

TABLE 3.1
Population and Sample Sizes and Sampling Ratios by Class

District	School	Class	Number of First Graders in Class	Number of First Graders Studied	Proportion of Class Studied
I	A	01	37	17	0.46
	B	02	35	13	0.37
		03	36	18	0.50
		04	15[a]	6	0.40
		05	35	8	0.23
II	C	06	20	6	0.30
		07	20	6	0.30
		08	19	7	0.37
	D	09	27	12	0.44
		10	27	8	0.30
III	E	11	28	7	0.25
		12	29	9	0.31
	F	13	37	8	0.22
		14	33	14	0.42
		15	36	8	0.22
Total			434	147	0.34

[a] Class 04 is a mixed first and second grade class containing 15 first and 15 second graders.

3.2). We describe these measures in some detail here although derived indices are discussed later at the points in the analyses where they appear.

Basic Evidence

Children's aptitude. Evidence on children's reading aptitude was obtained by administering the Word Learning Tasks (Barr 1971) consisting of a phonics and a sight word reading task. Each task, administered on separate days, involved teaching five words over a fifteen-minute period to groups of six children on one day, testing learning on five test trials, and checking for retention the following day on two test trials. The instructional methods of the two tasks were designed to resemble those used in the instruction of a phonics as well as the initial phase of an eclectic word-based reading approach. The total scores for learning and retention, derived from the phonics and sight word tasks, were combined to obtain an estimate of reading aptitude. Scores on the tasks ranged from 6 to a perfect score of 70. Scores in the range from 6 to 24 indicate low aptitude for reading; from 25 to 46, average aptitude; and from 47 to 70, high aptitude. Test-retest reliabilities of the *Word Learning Tasks* are high ($r = 0.91$ to 0.95). Predictive validity with reading at the end of first grade ($r = 0.62$ to $r = 0.68$) is similar to that of other readiness measures.

TABLE 3.2
EVIDENCE USED IN THE ANALYSIS

Condition	Source
Children's Aptitude	Word Learning Tasks
Children's Learning	Basal word learning
	Phonics learning
	Gates MacGinitie Reading Tests: Vocabulary
	Gates MacGinitie Reading Tests: Comprehension
Children's Background (sex, chronological age, socio-economic status)	School records
Class Size	Teacher report
Reading Group Membership	Teacher report
Material Difficulty—Basal	Examination of reading materials
Material Difficulty—Phonics	Examination of reading materials
Content Coverage—Basal	Teacher report
Content Coverage—Phonics	Teacher report
Daily Class Time	Weekly class schedule
Scheduled Reading Time	Weekly class schedule
Estimated Basal Time	Teacher report
Estimated Phonics Time	Teacher report
Teacher Experience	Teacher report

Children's learning. Two types of learning outcomes were measured: immediate learning specific to the content of the material taught, and general reading achievement, which is not directly tied to specific curricular content. The content-specific measure is useful because of its sensitivity to the effects of instructional conditions. The combination of the two measures allowed us to examine the contribution of specific content learning to the development of more general reading skills.

Two measures of content learning were included: one pertaining to basal words, the other to phonics. Basal word tests were designed for individual children and administered in December and May of first grade. A sample of at least 10 words—but usually about 20—was selected systematically using every *n*th word from those listed at the back of the readers. The word sample was the same for each child in a given basal reading series but varied in length according to the number of words that had been introduced. The selected words were shown to all children individually to determine the number they could pronounce. The proportion of words correctly identified was used to estimate the number of words learned by December and May of first grade. For example, if a child had been taught 100 words and correctly pronounced a test of 20 words selected from the set of 100, he or she would be assigned a score indicating that 100 had been learned.

Phonics learning was assessed by an informal test involving the pronunciation of syllables. The test contained fifteen items with an equal number of two-, three-, and four-letter syllables. It was scored on the basis of correctly pronounced phonemes and vowel markers. The test, administered to each child individually in May of first grade, is highly reliable ($r = 0.88$; split-half method).

General reading achievement was measured by the Gates-MacGinitie Reading Tests, Primary A, Form I, vocabulary and comprehension tests. These tests measure a variety of reading skills: the vocabulary section demands recognition of printed words occurring as isolated units that correspond to a picture; the comprehension section involves reading short passages in order to select a picture conveying the meaning. Coefficients of validity for the tests ranged from 0.60 to 0.86.

Background characteristics of children. Evidence of age, sex, and socioeconomic status was obtained from each child's school record during the autumn. Age was recorded in months as of September of first grade. Parental occupations were classified on a scale of 1 to 5: 1. unskilled and semiskilled; 2. skilled; 3. lower white collar; 4. upper white collar; 5. professional.

Class size and group membership. During the autumn, teachers reported the number of children in their classes, and this number was used as the index of class size. Although there was some mobility during the school year, children leaving classes were replaced by new class members so that the November estimates reflect the size during the remainder of the school year.

The reading group of each child in the sample was reported by teachers in December and May. These reports were used to determine the number of reading groups in each class as well as the group placement of children. As shown in table 3.5, the number of groups ranged from two to four in the fifteen classes.

Instructional materials. Reading programs typically include two types of materials: those to be read by teachers and those to be read by children. The teachers' materials include a guide to accompany the basal readers and an annotated edition of the student workbooks. The materials for children commonly include a series of basal readers containing stories of increasing difficulty and workbooks to accompany the readers with exercises to develop specific skills such as the use of context, comprehension strategies, structural analysis, and phonics analysis. In addition, teachers often supplement the workbook and story selections with blackboard activities, dittoed materials, storybooks, and writing activities. All these activities for children, with the exception of basal reading, we refer to collectively as *skill work.*

Reading programs are designed to reflect a general curricular plan of progressive conceptual development. The introduction of new concepts, however, typically proceeds in several areas simultaneously. For example, in beginning reading materials, stories increase in length, sentences in complexity, and questions in variety as children progress from reader to reader. The stories are characterized by the units of print such as the word or letter, which are controlled through gradual introduction over successive stories. In the workbooks, comprehension, structural, and phonics skills may also be introduced sequentially.

The concepts introduced in instructional materials may become increasingly complex or they may remain of similar difficulty. The latter seems to be true with beginning reading materials. It is hard to argue that the new words introduced in the fifteenth story are more difficult than those in the first; but the fifteenth story is more difficult because it includes not only its own new words, but those introduced in previous stories. Similarly, phonics concepts introduced in the third workbook are no harder than those introduced in the first; but because of accumulating knowledge about phonics, children can undertake more complicated forms of phonics analysis in the third workbook.

Reading materials vary in the number of new units introduced over the course of a grade level reading program. Whereas the first grade stories in one series, for example, might introduce a total of 350 new words over the year, a second series with a more gradual introduction of new words might include only 250. Similarly, one series might introduce many more phonics concepts than another. We refer to this as *material difficulty*.

The reading series used by classes in the six schools were developed so that a few new words would be introduced in each successive story and repeated in subsequent ones. Table 3.3 shows that the series were similar in the total number of names and sight words introduced (words to be memorized), but different in the total number of words to be analyzed. On the basis of the total number of new words introduced, schools C and D used slightly more difficult basal materials than schools A, B, E, and F (356 versus 324 words, respectively).

Information was also available on the number of phonics elements introduced. Schools A, B, C, D, and E used the workbook materials included in the basal reading program. By contrast, school F adopted an alternative skills program which emphasized phonics concepts to replace the seatwork materials that accompanied its basal program. The schools differed widely in the extent to which their materials introduced phonics elements. As table 3.4 shows, the workbooks used by schools A, B, and E introduced a total of forty-five phonics elements, most of which were consonants and consonant clusters. By contrast, schools C, D, and F used workbooks containing many more phonics elements, sixty-six and sixty-three, respectively, that pertained to vowel as well as consonant letter-sound associations. Accordingly, the phonics materials used by schools A, B, and E are easier than those of schools C, D, and F.

Content coverage. Not all first graders completed the materials. In early December and mid-May, teachers were asked to report how far along the children in each of their instructional groups were in their basal reading materials. By tabulating the reported page numbers, the number of word and phonics concepts encountered by each child in December and May could be determined. For example, if children had completed preprimer 3 in school A, their word content coverage (or pace) would be 72 (see table 3.3) and their phonics pace, 9 (see table 3.4). Children completing the third preprimer in school F would have the same basal word pace but a higher phonics pace of 35. We use the terms *content coverage* and *pace* interchangeably to refer to the number of units encountered within a specified time period. December pace pertains to the number of word or phonics units introduced during the first three months of instruction; May pace refers to those introduced over the nine-month school year.

Scheduled time measures. The basic data included daily class schedules and teacher interview reports on the use of time during reading instruction. From this evidence, several different measures of time were derived. *Daily time* is simply the length of time children spend in school from the beginning of class, excluding time for lunch, until dismissal.

TABLE 3.3
NUMBER OF STORIES AND NEW WORDS INCLUDED IN FIRST GRADE READING PROGRAMS

Level of Material	Program Used in Schools A, B, E, and F (Scott Foresman)				Level of Material	Program Used in Schools C and D (Macmillan)			
	Stories	Names and Sight Words	Words to Be Analyzed	Total New Words		Stories	Names and Sight Words	Words to Be Analyzed	Total New Words
Preprimer 1	11	18	0	18	Level 3	10	25	0	25
Preprimer 2	26	40	0	40	Level 4	21	44	1	45
Preprimer 3	44	72	0	72	Level 5	35	66	1	67
Primer	78	155	18	173	Primer	78	140	42	182
First Reader	114	258	66	324	First Reader	117	247	109	356

Note: Vertical columns represent cumulative frequencies.

TABLE 3.4
NUMBER OF PHONICS ELEMENTS INCLUDED IN FIRST GRADE READING PROGRAMS

Level of Material	Program Used in Schools A, B, and E (Scott Foresman)				Program Used in Schools C and D (Macmillan)				Program Used in School F (Reardon-Bear)			
	Consonants	Consonant Clusters	Word Endings	Vowels	Consonants	Consonant Clusters	Word Endings	Vowels	Consonants	Consonant Clusters	Word Endings	Vowels
Preprimer 1	0	0	0	0	11	0	3	0	15	0	0	0
Preprimer 2	5	0	0	0	15	0	3	0	20	0	2	2
Preprimer 3	9	0	0	0	17	0	9	0	20	0	7	8
Primer	16	1	5	0	18	4	15	5	20	12	9	10
First Reader	17	19	9	0	21	16	16	13	20	24	9	10

Note: Vertical columns represent cumulative frequencies.

The six schools were similar in total daily time, with only fifteen minutes separating schools A and B from the rest.

Classes differed considerably in *total time allocated to reading instruction*. As shown in table 3.5, school C and D teachers scheduled more time than the others. School B teachers scheduled the briefest amount, although teacher 03 allocated more time to reading than the others in the same school.

Teachers reported using scheduled time in different ways, and language arts as well as reading activities were included. Three organizational arrangements were common: total class instruction, small group instruction conjoined with minimally supervised seatwork, and supervised reading work. As table 3.5 shows, all teachers in schools A, B, C, and E and teacher 15 in school F reported that they typically began the reading period with total class instruction, and most, with the exception of school C teachers, used this time to introduce and discuss the skill work assignments to be completed by all class members as seatwork. School C teachers allocated more time to total class instruction and used about one-half of it to discuss basal story selections and the other half to develop skill work concepts.

All teachers used small group instruction accompanied by seatwork for the remainder of the class, but they differed on whether time in small groups was devoted to reading basal stories or to other skill work as well. They also used seatwork time in different ways, placing varying emphasis on workbooks, writing, and blackboard exercises as well as on stories and phonics.

In some classes, a third type of instructional arrangement followed either the total class or the combined small group–seatwork component: teacher supervised work. In some schools, this activity involved a seatwork arrangement, with the teacher circulating around the class and inspecting work to identify children needing special help and support. In others, supervised activities consisted of small groups of children reading stories taken from outdated basal series that used the same set of words as those introduced in the current basal series.

On the basis of the teacher descriptions of instruction and the daily schedules, we made estimates of the time allocated to basal reading and skill work during total class instruction, small group instruction, seatwork, and teacher supervised work. First, on the basis of teacher reports, we divided the time scheduled for reading and language arts into its component instructional arrangements (e.g., total class introduction of seatwork activities, small group reading instruction, supervised seatwork, and work check). Then we further divided the total time set aside for group instruction into portions allotted to each group and calculated the duration of small group reading and unsupervised seatwork time for each one. We assumed that all groups in a class received the same

TABLE 3.5
Total Reading Time and Time Allocated to Basal and Skill Work Activities in Total Class, Small Group, Seat Work, and Teacher Supervised Work Arrangements (Minutes)

School	Class	Number of May Groups	Total Time Allocated to Reading	Total Class Instr. Basal Reading	Total Class Instr. Skill Work	Small Group Instr. Basal Reading	Small Group Instr. Skill Work	Seat Work Basal Reading	Seat Work Skill Work	Teacher Superv. Work Basal Reading	Teacher Superv. Work Skill Work
A	01	3	120	0	15	25	10	0	70	0	0
B	02	4	90	0	10	20	0	0	60	0	0
	03	4	120	0	10	20	0	0	60	30	0
	04	2[a]	90	0	15	25	0	0	50	0	0
	05	3	90	0	15	25	0	0	50	0	0
C	06	2	150	30	30	15	15	10	20	10	20
	07	2	150	30	30	15	15	10	20	10	20
	08	2	150	30	30	15	15	10	20	10	20
D	09	3	150	0	0	30	10(40)[b]	30(0)[b]	80	0	0
	10	4	150	0	0	20	10	0	90	30	0
E	11	4	120	0	20	20	0	0	60	20	0
	12	3	120	0	30	20	0	0	40	30	0
F	13	2	120	0	0	20	20	20	20	10	30
	14	3	120	0	0	15	15	20	40	10	20
	15	2	120	0	30	20	10	20	10	10	20

[a] We have assumed that the second graders constituted a third instructional group in class 04.
[b] The low group in class 09 received extra small group instruction in skill work, while the remaining groups read from the basal reader and library books.

amount of small group time. Finally, we examined teacher descriptions of their reading instruction to judge the proportion of time in each instructional arrangement focused on basal story activities and on other reading and language skill work.

These time estimates are shown in table 3.5. For example, teacher 01 reported allocating about two hours to reading and related activities. A typical day began with about fifteen minutes of total class instruction in which special skill work assignments related to reading and language arts were discussed. Then during the remaining time, each of three groups met in turn with the teacher for about thirty-five minutes, during which most of the time was spent on basal reading and about ten minutes on skill work exercises. The seatwork time of about seventy minutes (occurring at the same time as small group instruction) consisted of skill work assigned during total class and small group instruction. On the basis of the teacher's description of reading activities, we estimated that approximately twenty-five minutes of instructional time were devoted to basal activity and a total of ninety-five minutes to skill work activity. Basal and skill work time estimates for groups of students in other classes were determined in the same way.

Total reading, basal, and skill work time must be considered as outside limits on available time. No allowance is made for transitional events and other intrusions that typically reduce the amount of time available for instruction. Similarly, time for preparation and other nonreading events is not considered. Further, during seatwork, it is well established that not all children use all available time productively and that some children complete assigned work long before the end of a work period. The estimates of allocated time therefore should not be misinterpreted as measures of actual time devoted to reading.

Teacher experience. We had no direct evidence of teacher proficiency. In lieu of refined measures, the number of years each teacher had taught first grade was used to measure direct experience with first grade instruction. Table 3.6 shows that teachers in the fifteen classes varied from having had no prior first grade experience (teachers 04, 05, 09, and 11) to having had extensive experience (teacher 03).

Evaluation of the Evidence

As stated earlier, the characteristics of the evidence made it particularly useful for the purpose of secondary analysis. The selection of schools and classes permitted us to compare cases within levels and to conduct analyses across them, although the absence of a second class within school A mars the overall design.

The sampling of individuals within schools yielded sufficient numbers of children to estimate the characteristics of classes with confidence. However, the size of the samples precluded our examining the distrib-

TABLE 3.6
Years of First Grade Teaching Experience

School	Class	Experience Teaching First Grade
A	01	7
B	02	6
	03	19
	04	0
	05	0
C	06	0
	07	4
	08	1
D	09	0
	10	3
E	11	0
	12	1
F	13	1
	14	4
	15	3

utive properties of instructional groups, although measures of size and central tendency were obtained. While the numbers of children studied were sufficient for our purposes of exploring instructional groups, they did not permit us to draw firm conclusions about group organization. This problem does not, however, interfere with our analyses of individual learning, although unequal numbers of students representing classes and groups may result in certain combinations of conditions being over-represented in the individual analysis, thereby biasing the results.

The basic evidence is of excellent quality, with certain exceptions. Student aptitude, learning, and background characteristics, difficulty of instructional materials, and content coverage are validly and reliably measured. Although class size, reading group membership, daily class time, scheduled reading time, and teacher experience reflect reliable teacher reports, we would have preferred more direct measures of time and teacher proficiency based on direct observation. And while we have some reservations about their adequacy as absolute measures, we have confidence that they are serviceable relative measures, which is all the present argument calls for. We advise the reader to treat the empirical results concerning time with caution, but to have considerable confidence in those pertaining to aptitude, instructional material difficulty, content coverage, and learning.

Organization of the Evidence

Three sets of evidence were created corresponding to the class, group, and individual levels of school system organization. The individual set was the most extensive because students were described not only by their unique characteristics (aptitude, sex, learning, age) but also by those of their instructional group (content coverage, estimated time) and their class (teacher experience, instructional material difficulty, total reading time). Correspondingly, the group set was the next most extensive, including not only group measures but also class indices.

In addition, certain characteristics of individuals were aggregated to characterize groups and classes, and properties of groups were combined to describe classes. For example, instructional groups were described by the average aptitude of group members, and classes by the number of instructional groups as well as by the aptitude distribution of class members. We describe more precisely the measures of group and class properties when they are discussed later in the text.

RESOURCE ALLOCATION AND LEARNING

Having devised a formulation for understanding how schools work, shown its derivation, and described the methods of investigation, we turn now to an empirical examination of the social organization of school production. All forms of production involve mobilizing resources in different parts of an organization to create some value; and school systems are no different. From the conventional viewpoint, the value schools are supposed to produce is individual learning: that is what parents, teachers, community interest groups, and the students themselves intend. Indeed, students do learn in schools; and those who investigate the effectiveness of schooling inquire into the conditions that lead to different amounts of learning. In a sense, they proceed backward from the product.

Without subordinating the importance of individual learning, we suggest that the reason it varies can be approached differently. Schooling takes place in large organizations, much of whose energy and resources are engaged in just operating. With this in mind, we can think of individual learning as one among several products. And while it may represent the prime justification for the existence of schools, in the process of establishing "social relations of production," connections between their internal parts are necessarily created as well as outcomes peculiar to those parts. Here we think about school production forwards by inquiring into the nature of the organization, its parts, their outcomes, and the concatenation of events that leads finally to learning.

An organization runs on resources, and how it works depends on what happens to them. While we cannot examine every resource, we do treat three of the four we identified earlier as prevailing conditions of classroom instruction: its students, instructional materials, and time. The first and most fundamental condition a teacher must deal with in establishing an instructional program is the class: the number of children present (class size) and the distribution of their aptitudes (reading readiness). Large numbers of children are often considered by teachers to be a liability, making it harder to carry on instruction; but that is not assuredly the case, because instructional difficulty may depend on the aptitudes of the students, not necessarily on the size of the class. Size in fact represents the aggregate number of student contributions to the classroom enterprise. Because instruction entails the adaptation of teachers' time and talents along with material resources to what children are capable of doing, the distribution of children's aptitudes as well as their number is considered. Educational production, unlike manufacture, is not a process by which raw materials are passively shaped. It entails the active participation of students, a prime component of which is their capacity to do the work.

Learning materials such as books and worksheets are the main physical resources that support learning to read. We argue that the most important attribute of instructional materials is their difficulty because they must be adjusted to children's capabilities. Extremely difficult materials are inappropriate because they lead to frustration and little learning; extremely easy materials present no challenge. One might argue instead that the content, organization, and emphasis of materials are what is really important. But these properties pertain more to matters of curricular priority than to instructional activity, which in the nature of the case must come to terms with what children are able to do. Material difficulty is most relevant, therefore, because it is tied up instructionally with aptitude. And while it is important to know the difficulty of the materials that a teacher has available, it is even more important to know how they are used. The condition of interest here is children's exposure to learning materials over time, or content coverage.

Finally, time represents a central condition of instruction. Obviously if very little time is available, not much instruction can transpire. Time places an outer limit on possible instruction, but having time does not automatically translate into viable instruction.

When a set of instructional conditions has been identified, the usual way to determine their connection to learning is to add up their combined effects through multiple regression analysis. This procedure assumes, of course, that the algebraic addition implicit in the statistical technique adequately represents educational production; that production itself entails adding together at the margin different resources in the right quantities. We argue that production does not necessarily have such additive properties and that it needs to be described in more substantive terms.

At least three things need to be known about productive resources: first, where they originate—in what part, or hierarchical level, of the organization do they enter the productive process; second, how much they vary at each level, for if they do not vary, it is exceedingly difficult to detect their influence on outcomes; and third, what happens to them as they get moved from level to level, for if resources are actually used in production, we should expect to find them transformed, consumed, or changed in their manifestations. To address these questions, one cannot assume that resources can simply be enumerated and added up. Rather, it is necessary to trace their distribution at each level of school system organization to identify where each resource is found, how it is distributed, and whether the distribution changes from one level to another.

Consider the case of the number of students. The number of school-age children is a characteristic of a community's population; it changes gradually in response to conditions most of which are beyond the control of the district administration. Within a district, however, the size of schools is largely a function of how the school board and superintendent draw school boundaries as well as of decisions by members of households about where to live. Determining the size of classes falls within the jurisdiction of the school principal, but is hedged about with constraints. Some schools in our sample show marked differences in class size, so that exploring some reasons for size disparity should shed light on how this numerical resource is allocated.

The signs of deliberate allocative decisions appear in schools C and D, both located in the same district and hence subject to the same district policies. The two schools have similar numbers of first graders, fifty-nine and fifty-four, respectively. The principal of school C assigned the fifty-nine children to three teachers, giving each class an enrollment of about twenty. In school D, fifty-four children are assigned to only two teachers in classes of twenty-seven each. Why the large disparity in class size? The most likely reason is that the district sets a ceiling on class size. If the ceiling is twenty-eight, school C has too many children (59) and so is entitled to an additional teacher if the classes are not to contain 29 and 30 children and thus be oversubscribed. School D does not have enough first graders to justify an additional teacher. If district standards are not entailed in this kind of allocation decision, however, then we need to know why two principals in the same district form classes of such different size. But we do not. A surplus or deficit of children sometimes gets resolved not by the creation of class size disparities between schools but by the establishment of mixed-grade classes within a school. Class 04 in school B is such a case: it combines able first graders with slow second graders, a very difficult combination to instruct.

The size of classes is also influenced simply by the number of children enrolled in the grade. In the inner city district, all classes are large, ranging from thirty to thirty-seven; and in the suburban district III, one school has class enrollments of twenty-eight and twenty-nine while another ranges between thirty-three and thirty-seven. Class size is moderately related to grade size ($r = 0.57$; $p < 0.05$), which is a school property. But it also appears to be determined by district-wide decision rules and undoubtedly by the principal acting within the range of administrative discretion.

As we will show in detail in the next chapter, not only do the groups teachers divide classes into for reading instruction differ in size but also their relative size changes over the course of the year as instruction proceeds and teachers gauge its results. Thus, from district to school to class to instructional group, one can observe the progressive reduction in size of the groupings that constitute the levels of school system organization. But simply to find a direct relation between hierarchical level and size of grouping is not very important. One should think instead about district and school administrators and teachers, located at different hierarchical levels, each facing a different kind of numerical problem: district administrators allocating a district-wide school population to separate schools by defining catchment areas, school administrators assigning students in each school to classes so that the class distribution of children's characteristics is established, and teachers arranging classes into groups that are appropriate in size for instruction.

In a sense, this discussion of the size of units is artificial because decisions cannot be made about size alone detached from other considerations. For unless the population of a school district is completely homogeneous—which is never the case—decisions about size by necessity entail decisions about the distributions of children's characteristics. Decisions about the allocation of resources are actually interlocking, and a decision made about one necessarily entails decisions about others at the same time. They are mutually constraining, but nevertheless have to be discussed one at a time.

In accord with our interest in the nature of classroom instruction, resources that bear strongly on instruction are of paramount concern. One of these, obviously, is the aptitude of individual children, for this is a capacity that both influences what they will learn and represents a condition toward which teachers orient instruction. This means that they take into account both individual capacities and the distribution of those capacities, the latter to determine how the class should be arranged for instruction. Our immediate interest, however, is in how the class distribution of aptitudes got to be there in the first place. Just as the school-age population of a district can be viewed as a pool of individuals successively divided into smaller aggregates in accordance with the agendas of each level of organization, we can think of a district-wide distribution of children's aptitudes as a pool of resources that gets reallocated as children are assigned to schools, to classes, and to instructional groups. We can then inspect the properties of these distributions of resources.

The three districts in our sample, even though they differ markedly in community socioeconomic status, are very similar in their distributions of aptitude: about eight points separate the means of the highest and lowest, and about two points separate their standard deviations (see appendix A). We cannot vouch for the six schools being representative samples of their respective districts. The mean and standard deviation differences across schools within districts are no larger than the differences between districts, whereas if schools had been randomly selected, there is reason to believe that standard deviations within districts might have been larger. Caution must be exercised in interpreting these findings because district and school differences are artifacts of the sampling, and the full range of differences between schools in each district may not be represented. The most interesting observation, however, is that such socioeconomically different communities overlap so much in their district and school distributions of aptitude.

When we proceed to the class level, we find some schools where the aptitude distribution of classes is alike and others where it differs. But with the exception of school F (in which the classes are administratively designed to differ by ability), whose highest and lowest classes differ by twenty points, the classes in all other schools do not differ by more than twelve aptitude points, a difference not much greater than that separating the highest and lowest districts.

Within the confines of our sampled districts and schools, it appears that the successive assignment of children to schools and classes does not alter in fundamental ways the mean level of aptitudes or their dispersion. What does change, however, is the skewness of aptitude both in schools and in classes, a point we shall return to in chapter 4. For the most part, then, we can think of the assignment of children to schools and classes as a kind of transmission process in which the properties of the district-wide distribution remain largely unchanged. The distribution is not transformed to reveal different properties—with the exception of its symmetry related to the appearance of several classes with large positive skew.

At the instructional group level, however, a massive transformation in aptitude distribution transpires. It is no less dramatic for being expected with the appearance of reading groups, a familiar element in the teaching of first grade reading. Except in the three classes that start with only one group, the difference in mean aptitude between the highest and lowest group ranges from about twelve to fifty-one, and in seven classes the difference is thirty points or more (see appendix B). By contrast, school and class differences are relatively minor when compared with differences between groups within classes, an observation that may account for why school and class comparisons have in the past provided weak and inconsistent explanations for variation in learning.

Finally, at the level of individual children, groups differ in the homogeneity of aptitude. In some it is very broad, in others narrow; but on the whole, we found more variation in groups around class means than individual variation around group means—exactly what one would expect if grouping is designed to reduce individual variation in the service of establishing teachable aggregations of children.

Unlike the transmission process that occurs between the district and class levels, a major differentiation inside classes takes place in which both the size of the aggregation changes and the nature of the aptitude distribution itself changes. By the end of the year, this has occurred in all classes even though we find some variations on this general theme: in school C, where group formation is delayed; and in school F, where the classes themselves are distinguished by ability and also grouped internally. But whatever the particulars, we observe a change in organizational pattern, as indicated by the transformation of the aptitude distribution, at the location in the school system where instructional activities transpire: in groups, not in schools or in classes. This suggests that in primary school reading, the classroom is not per se the organizational unit of instruction, a point we will develop fully in chapter 4.

Awareness of the general problem of internal school variation has been with us for a long time. Jencks, for example, reminds us in his comments on the Coleman report that "the range of variation [in test performance] within the typical Northern urban elementary school was about 90 percent of the range for the urban North as a whole" (1972, p. 86). Yet there has been the failure to consider what needs to be known about internal variation and what aspects of it must be attended to. In our view, one needs to know at what organizational levels most of the variation in resources occurs. Knowing this makes it possible to determine which resources are differentially distributed and applied.

Earlier attempts to address the problem of within-school variation, as indicated in chapter 2, examined the direct effects of district, school, and class conditions on learning by expressing them as individual characteristics and experiences. This is a statistically feasible thing to do because all variation in schooling conditions can in fact be treated at the individual level, although often at the conceptual cost of misspecifying them. The result, however, is that what begins as an examination of school influences on learning becomes one of individual status attainment; for as with Jencks, it is the explanation of observed variation in individual test results (outcome measures) that sets the conceptual agenda. Is it not then natural to attribute these results to variations in school characteristics expressed as individual experiences but not as organizational properties?

Our analysis shows that aptitude can be treated differently. The fact that most of the variation in aptitude occurs between instructional groups within classes immediately signifies that we are dealing with an organizational phenomenon—a problem of class and group organization—as much as if not more than with a problem of individual attainment. That organizational phenomenon is the differentiation of classes into groups to manage the diversity of children's aptitudes. At the district, school, and class levels, there are no attempts to create organizational devices to manage this variation (with the partial exception of grade-wide grouping in school F). In secondary schools, however, one does find tracks—a school level device—and vocational schools—a district level device—to manage large variations in aptitude, interest, and future educational plans.

At the point where instruction takes place, where resources such as time, materials, and teachers' capacities are brought to bear directly upon children, we find an organizational response: group formation within classrooms. If children were randomly assigned to groups from the total class distribution, we would have reason to think of grouping as part of the allocative transmission process that begins at the district level and consists of the assignment of children to schools and classes. But at the group level we find one of those qualitative breaks in organizational structure which alerts us to important events in the productive process.

While there is every reason to believe that instruction occurs inside classrooms, the resources consumed in the course of instruction do not necessarily originate there. A proper examination of instruction requires considering how events happening in various parts of the school system make it possible for instruction to transpire where it does. In doing this, we turn to a systematic and quantitative analysis of how four resources—aptitude, time, materials, and coverage—all aspects of instruction, are distributed among districts, schools, classes, groups, and individuals, and how they are related to three individual measures of learning—basal word learning, reading vocabulary, and reading comprehension.

There are special difficulties in analyzing the impact of resources on individual learning, especially when we know that resource distributions are properties of the organization itself and not of individual children. Consider the case of associating variations in aptitude with those in learning. Children obviously differ in aptitude. But in the preceding discussion, we showed that aptitude also varies by district, school, class, and group. When correlating aptitude with learning, both as characteristics of individuals, one in fact treats variation in aptitude attributable to district, school, class, group, *and* individual influences. These multiple sources of aptitude variation are compressed into a global indication of experience, expressed as individual aptitude, that influences learning directly. All of these potentially independent sources of aptitude variation remain unidentified by source but are tacitly included in a confounded measure. In short, the measure of individual aptitude conceals several other sources of aptitude variation.

Because instructional conditions expressed as individual experiences are indeed differentiated according to source, we attempt here to identify the resources constituting instruction at their respective levels of organization. That is to say, while we have reason to believe that children's aptitudes influence their learning, we need to know whether a given instructional resource is attributable to a child's placement in a particular group, to aptitude differences among groups, to the preferences of different teachers in the same school as expressed in varying class-to-class grouping arrangements, to differences among schools in the same district, or to differences among districts. And likewise for the other three resources.

Most studies of educational production are designed within the confines of only one level of organization; they examine, for example, the impact of school or of class characteristics on learning. When relations are found, the school or class is then thought to have produced the outcome. And they might well have, but perhaps spuriously or in combination with other productive influences having other origins. Similarly, when relations are not found, it is sometimes assumed that the school or class has had no impact when in fact the impact is obscured because sought at the wrong level. Indeed, we have heard much in recent years about schools having trivial effects on learning.

Instead of examining the relation between individual aptitude and learning in a global fashion, we partitioned aptitude variation for each individual into five component scores: the difference between the individual score and group mean (individual), between the group and class mean (group), between the class and school mean (class), between the school and district mean (school), and between the district and grand mean (district). Each of these scores was then added to the set of data characterizing individuals. The partitioning of aptitude variation allows us to identify the organizational levels with which major portions of the variation are associated and to determine the impact of each source of variation on learning.

Consider first the case of aptitude (reading readiness) and its relation to the outcomes of reading instruction as shown in table 3.7. The first panel shows that the mean aptitude of all 147 children is 38. (Note that we have set the means for each partition equal to zero.) The total amount of variation around the grand mean of the whole sample, as indicated by the standard deviation, is 19. The table goes on to show how much variation in aptitude is attributable to each organizational level expressed respectively by standard deviations around each mean of zero. Consistent with the earlier discussion of aptitude distribution and resource transmission, the table shows only small amounts of aptitude variation at the class, school, and district levels (st. dev. = 5, 3, and 3, respectively). Substantially larger amounts of variation obtain at both the individual and group levels (st. dev. = 11 and 13, respectively). The first panel also shows healthy zero-order correlations between individual aptitude and the three measures of learning in the column containing individual variations around the grand mean of all 147 cases.

The body of the table presents correlations between aptitude, partitioned by level, and the three measures of learning. Most striking about them is the fact that they appear dramatically strong *at the group level* (r = 0.69, 0.65, and 0.69; p < 0.001), not at the individual level (r = 0.05, 0.15, and 0.17), despite the fact that individual aptitude within groups varies almost as much as group aptitude within classes, and despite the fact that the zero-order (unpartitioned) correlations are substantial. In sum, the zero-order correlations in fact represent variation occurring predominantly between groups and to a much lesser extent between individuals, between classes, between schools, and between districts.

These findings, that instructional group and not individual differences in aptitude have such a substantial association with learning, confound intuition. They do, however, locate the impact of aptitude precisely where instructional activity takes place—in classrooms—and to a much lesser extent in the capacities of individuals or in the form of the aggregate resources of classes, schools, and districts, which in more familiar terms would be called "climate."

The importance of locating the effect of aptitude on learning in groups is further substantiated when we turn attention to a major instructional condition, the coverage of basal reading materials over time (instructional pace), which we have partitioned in a similar fashion. The mean number of basal words covered by all children is 229 with a standard deviation of 100 as shown in panel 2 of table 3.7. Mean coverage at each level is again set to zero. There can be no variation in coverage among individuals because pace by definition is a group property with all individuals in each group covering the same amount of material in the same time.

There are three striking findings in the second panel of table 3.7. The first is the very substantial relation between the instructional condition of pace and learning. The second is that most of this variation (st. dev. = 82) appears at the group level (as is true with aptitude), even though substantial amounts of it also appear at the class, school, and district levels. The third is that the magnitude of correlations between content coverage and learning is proportional to the amount of variation in coverage, and perforce the association of pace with learning is greatest at the group level.

The fact that variation in coverage also occurs above the instructional group level does not necessarily mean that it is actually established in

TABLE 3.7

Total Variation and Variation Partitioned by Organizational Level for Aptitude, Content Coverage (Pace), Material Difficulty, and Allocated Time; and Correlation Coefficients Showing the Relation between Components of Variation and Learning, for Basal Instruction (n = 147)

| Schooling Conditions | Means and S.D.s of Conditions; and Learning | Correlation Coefficients between Conditions and Learning | | | | | | |
| | | Total | Partitioned Deviations by Level | | | | | |
		Indiv. around Grand Mean	Indiv. around Group Means	Group around Class Means	Class around School Means	School around District Means	District around Grand Mean
Children's Aptitude	Mean	38	0	0	0	0	0
	Standard deviation	19	11	13	5	3	3
	Basal word learning	.60**	.05	.69**	.18	.22*	.02
	Reading vocabulary	.68**	.15	.65**	.16	.18	.33**
	Reading comprehension	.69**	.17	.69**	.20*	.16	.16
Content Coverage (pace)	Mean	229	0	0	0	0	0
	Standard deviation	100	0	82	42	17	34
	Basal word learning	.93**	—	.75**	.40**	.17	.29**
	Reading vocabulary	.73**	—	.65**	.29**	.14	.15
	Reading comprehension	.73**	—	.64**	.24*	.15	.22*
Material Difficulty	Mean	333	0	0	0	0	0
	Standard deviation	14	0	0	0	0	14
	Basal word learning	.29**	—	—	—	—	.29**
	Reading vocabulary	.24*	—	—	—	—	.24*
	Reading comprehension	.26**	—	—	—	—	.26**
Time Allocated to Instruction	Mean	44	0	0	0	0	0
	Standard deviation	15	0	0	8	3	12
	Basal word learning	.34**	—	—	.34**	-.15	.22*
	Reading vocabulary	.44**	—	—	.26**	-.01	.36**
	Reading comprehension	.35**	—	—	.19	-.04	.28**

* p < 0.01, one-tailed test. ** p < 0.001, one-tailed test.

a productive sense at those other levels. Class variation most likely reflects teacher preferences or expertise in managing reading instruction that pertains to all reading groups in a class; accordingly the effect is actually established at the group level. Further, it is highly likely that the district variation reflects not district policy about pacing but rather district considerations in the procurement of instructional materials, which themselves influence pace, a point we will treat in chapter 5 when discussing the relation between the difficulty of materials and pace.

This analysis, it should be noted, does not indicate why effects appear at one level or another or how they come about. It does, however, provide useful clues to where productive processes might actually occur. A study, for instance, that compares the effects of schools might—erroneously—conclude that pace has but a minor impact on learning; a compounding of that error would lead to the misleading conclusion that differences between schools are unimportant. The small correlations between pace and learning (ranging from 0.14 to 0.17) at the school level suggest not the ineffectuality of schools but rather that the impact of schools may occur through events taking place in classes and in instructional groups. But one can only reach this conclusion by inspecting the whole partitioned analysis.

We are now in a better position to understand why aptitude variation at the group, but not at the individual, level is so strongly associated with learning. It is because a major component of instruction, the coverage of material over time, is organized around groups; and as we will show in chapter 4, aptitude forms the basis of their establishment. We find preliminary indications from this analysis, particularly from the miniscule association between individual aptitude and learning, that teachers attend more to the *distribution of aptitude* in a class and its transformation into instructible groups than to the particular aptitudes of individual children. Their instructional activity, in particular how much material they cover, is geared to groups and not to individuals. At the same time, it would be silly to deny the importance of aptitude as an influence upon learning. Indeed, our analysis shows aptitude and pace to have collinear effects at the group level; and when total variation is considered at the individual level, correlations between aptitude and learning are substantial, ranging from 0.60 to 0.69 (table 3.7, panel 1).

Turning to the remaining two resources in the third and fourth panels, the nature of materials and time allocated to instruction, we find different patterns. Partitioned variation in the difficulty of learning materials appears only at the district level and undoubtedly reflects district procurement policy. Within districts, all schools, classes, and groups then use essentially the same basal reading materials, the process of allocative transmission being direct and without qualitative distinction by level. Relative to content coverage, total variation in time appears primarily at the district level and to a lesser extent at the school and class levels reflecting overall time allotments as matters of district policy, which establishes daily time limits, as well as school scheduling and teacher time preferences. We would expect to see more variation at the class and group levels if we had measures of *actual* time used for basal instruction rather than scheduled time. Neither scheduled time nor the difficulty of materials shows associations with learning as large as those found for aptitude and coverage.

We summarize the most important findings. First, when we partition by level the variation in resources used in instruction—aptitude, coverage, material, and time—only in the case of aptitude does any variation appear at the individual level and this despite the fact that all the resources have a statistically significant association with learning when total variation is considered. Second, variation in these resources manifests itself at different hierarchical locations; and the patterns we find are consistent with the nature of the special agendas of each level. Third, the magnitude of associations between resources and learning depends on how much each resource varies. When there is only a little variation, the associations are necessarily small. But when the variation is substantial, the size of the association can be large or small. Indeed, the latter was tellingly the case when aptitude and learning were only negligibly associated even though there was substantial variation in individual aptitudes around group means. Fourth, aptitude is important not only as an indication of individual capacity for learning but as an organizational resource that is transformed by turning the aggregate of children in a classroom into instructible units. Fifth, aptitude and the coverage of material, each very well measured in this study, are strongly associated not only with learning content specific to the curriculum (basal words learned) but with learning as measured by standardized tests (vocabulary and comprehension) which do not reflect curricular content as faithfully. And finally, the level at which the analysis is pitched will determine what one finds.

With respect to the final point: the partitioned analysis clearly demonstrates the consequences of correctly and incorrectly specifying school system conditions. If we had examined the coverage of basal materials as the basis of school comparisons in learning, the impact of coverage would have appeared trivial; that would also have been true if time allocated to basal instruction had been treated as a property of schools. Consequently, identifying conditions of learning at some higher level than where they actually vary the most fails to represent properly their contributions to learning. Equally as important, considering variation only at the individual level fails to identify the levels within the school system at which variation occurs.

A parallel argument holds for learning outcomes. If, for example, only school means in learning are considered, the chances of identifying class and group conditions decrease. Only to the extent that the effects of lower level conditions are pervasive will they become manifest in variation between schools (for example, if variation internal to schools is minimal). Indeed, conditions may operate specifically within one level—not necessarily the school level—and still be extremely important. Coverage, of course, is a good case in point. Accordingly, the aggregation of learning outcomes to the school level biases findings toward the identification of productive conditions at that level and against their discovery at lower levels.

The existence of distinct organizational levels in school systems increases the difficulty of discovering the effectiveness of conditions conducive to learning. Appropriate identification of their effects can only occur when they are specified according to organizational level and when there is variation in outcomes sensitive to those conditions. We must know enough about the productive workings to identify accurately the location of their influence. A condition that is actually the accumulation of several influences originating at various places in a school system—an inappropriately global measure—precludes a test of its real impact. Such aggregated outcome measures may conceal the variation needed to trace the impact of educational conditions on learning correctly.

While we promised in chapter 1 to treat the distinct organizational agendas of school systems at their respective levels, we have not yet delivered on that promise—but will shortly. Instead, we have taken the first step in showing that it is worth keeping. The previous analysis was carried out at the individual level only, but it provides persuasive evidence that there are indeed different sorts of things happening at each level. At best, it provides an armature around which an analysis of class organization, group instruction, and their impact on learning can be built. While we have reason to suspect, for example, that groups are organized on the basis of aptitude and that the pace of instruction is tied to grouping, we have not yet shown *how* these conditions are tied up with each other to constitute the internal workings of a school. We know, moreover, that learning materials are brought into the school system at the district level. Everyone recognizes that they are used in classrooms and in instructional groups, but we have not yet undertaken to show how. In sum, it is better to know where resources enter the system and how much they vary than not to, but it is better still to know how they are conjoined to constitute school production. We turn now to this latter question, and in the next chapter discuss how the distribution of aptitudes in classrooms gets tranformed into instructible grouping arrangements.

4. Social Organization of Classroom Instruction

       A formulation of classroom instruction should identify the forms of instructional activity, the events that constitute it, and their extension over time. But what should be observed to understand how instruction works? One answer is *students* because students learn; they are the direct beneficiaries of instruction, however much they actually benefit. This answer leads to questions about how much time they spend working, how much time they spend with the teacher, what is their motivation; and about their experience with learning materials and in different classroom arrangements.

       A second answer is *teachers* because teachers instruct. This leads to questions about their style of management, the nature of their discourse, and the way they ask questions, explain, sanction, supervise, and the like.

       A third answer is *activities*, the joint engagement of teachers and students in carrying out curricular tasks, where activities include patterns of interaction, aspects of class organization, curriculum content, and the intellectual and social demands made by the nature of the schoolwork itself.

       All of these are eminently plausible answers even though the apposite research does not inspire confidence. Beyond that, these answers are

conceptually questionable. Perspectives on instruction that stress individual experiences conducive to learning have largely ignored the organization of the classroom. Those that emphasize teaching have treated
the characteristics and actions of teachers to be the same thing as class
organization thus confounding teacher activities with the setting in which
they occur. And those concentrating on activities have typically mixed
class, group, social interaction, individual actions, and curricular demands in an undifferentiated conceptual jumble.

At this juncture, we find that a clear delineation of organizational
levels—school, class, group, and individual—and the events that occur
at each of them helps to sort out the elements of classroom instruction
and establish connections among them. We need to ask: What is the
nature of events occurring at each of these levels? It is perforce inappropriate to fasten on particular levels singly or to treat events occurring
at several levels indiscriminately without tying them down to their organizational origins.

We will argue that the primary agenda of class level events is to
establish a grouping arrangement in a class so that instruction can be
undertaken. Teachers arrange classes in different ways by dividing them
into groups, by setting each student to work independently, or by bringing all students together for a single activity. The purpose of these arrangements is to order students appropriately (in the teacher's eyes) so
that instructional activities can then take place.

Once a class arrangement has been established, instruction can begin.
Instruction, however, is a set of *activities oriented to the groups* established
through the arrangement. Consider the illustration of grouped instruction commonly found in first grade reading. A teacher creates reading
groups and then instructs them by having children read aloud and answer questions about stories. These activities are premised on the teacher
having planned earlier for the group, provided appropriate textual materials, and set priorities for what skills to impart and for how much
time to spend. Not only must this be done separately for each reading
group that meets in its turn, but the teacher must provide instruction
for the remainder of the class, usually by an assignment that can be
managed by children independently and with only perfunctory supervision.

Instruction, then, entails the mixing of teacher and student abilities
as well as materials over a period of time for groupings of children. And
in the instance of grouped instruction, the class is divided into a small,
intensive, teacher-driven component and a less intensive, largely self-
paced individual seatwork component which succeed each other over
time.

Comparing whole class with grouped instruction helps to clarify the
distinction between a class arrangement and the instruction of groups.

In grouped instruction, the class is divided into visible parts, each one of which is then instructed. The difference between the class itself and the instructional group is palpable. In what is commonly and confusingly known as whole class instruction, the class is arranged as one single group that includes all children. That unit is then given instruction, recitation being a prime example. There is an optical and conceptual illusion that confuses the whole class, a classroom level entity, with the plenary group which is a unit of instruction. Although they both contain the same number of children, they do not have the same meaning organizationally. We must distinguish the class and its distributive properties from instructional entities which are derived from class properties, for the class itself is never a unit of instruction while a group the same size as the class can be.

In sum, classes are characteristically, though not exclusively, transformed into three types of arrangement: plenary aggregations, groups, and individually distinct members. These arrangements are respectively exposed to whole class, grouped, and individualized instruction which by definition takes place at the group level of organization. Note that we have used the term "group" here in a specialized—we trust not Pickwickian—way. When reading groups are employed, no stretching of the imagination is required in order to recognize that arrangement as grouped; even when whole class instruction is employed, that too can be readily understood as involving a very large group—one the size of the class itself. The contrasting limiting case is the thirty individual groups in a class of thirty receiving individualized instruction.

Classes of thirty, then, can be divided into single groups of thirty, thirty groups of one, and a variety of other combinations in between, such as three groups of ten. One must keep in mind that these groups are units of classroom organization (unlike classes, which are units of school organization) defined at an organizational level distinct from classes and located lower down in the school hierarchy. Conceptually, there is a world of difference between a class of thirty and an instructional group of thirty even when—indeed, especially when—they are both composed of the same children and the same teacher.

To round out the discussion, we note here the third aspect of classroom instruction: the individual student. To class arrangements and instructional activities designed for groups, children add their own abilities, interests, motivations, maturity, and perseverance and as a result learn. The situations of individual children and their resultant experiences are thus seen to be defined by class and group events as well as by the capacities that the children themselves bring to school.

In common usage, classroom instruction refers to all the things we have just described, but that usage conflates things that need to be distinguished. Note, too, that we have given instruction a technical meaning referring to activities directed toward groups established within classes. To understand classroom organization, the first question must be asked about the class, not about the children as individual learners, not about activities. The reason is that the teacher must do something about the class, arrange it in some way so that instruction can begin. Once an arrangement has been established, the teacher then engages in instructional activities with the groupings created by the arrangement.

GROUPING

While elementary school reading instruction usually employs ability grouping, grouping itself is part of the larger agenda of creating aggregations of students that are susceptible to instruction. Medieval schools, for example, according to Ariès, were characterized by "the lack of gradation in the curriculum according to difficulty of the subject-matter, the simultaneity with which the subjects were taught, the mixing of the ages, and the liberty of the pupils" (1962, p. 145). In due course, new institutions such as elementary schools appeared, and higher level schools became more internally differentiated. While we now take the age-graded school for granted, it is a relatively recent development. In the United States, graded schools appeared in the 1840s with "complaints about the difficulty of managing classes that contained a promiscuous assemblage of infants, boys, girls, large boys, big girls, young men and young women" (Kett 1977, p. 124). It also appeared in response to the feminization of teaching and to the financial economies attending it. "As long as schools were ungraded, it was difficult to justify the widespread use of female teachers, mainly because of doubts that tender ladies of 16 could manage plowboys of 18 in a classroom. Gradation, on the other hand, would permit the year-round employment of women, with older boys placed in high schools under male tutelage" (p. 125). Indeed, the classroom was an invention that replaced both the medieval schools and the later Lancastrian system with their large assemblages of students instructed at one time.

In the course of time, different aspects of the social grouping of classes became problematic for teachers: the size of the aggregation, its diversity in students' social and intellectual maturity, and the extent to which students possessed prior mastery of certain skills required by the curriculum. Various forms of ability grouping and tracking emerged in response to the problem of class and school diversity. For reasons difficult to explain, however, there appears to have been much greater interest in how grades get divided into classes than in how classes get divided into instructional groups. In both cases, moreover, the overriding question has been whether individual children assigned to homogeneously or heterogeneously composed classes or groups learn more.

Characteristic studies of grouping compare the learning of high ability children assigned to homogeneous classes to that of children of similar ability assigned to heterogeneous classes; and so on for average and low ability classes and children. This kind of design does not tell us about the nature of grouping, only about levels of individual performance related to membership in classes distinguished by ability in a grade or in groups distinguished by ability in a class.

Many studies indicate that grouping, presumably established to create more homogeneous classes than would appear if random class assignment were used, still results in considerable heterogeneity. Internal class diversity has been expressed as a problem of class overlap (Burr 1931), but this designation directs attention away from the instructional difficulties of teaching classes with wide ranges of ability and toward the assignment of children in a grade to the appropriate class, the latter being more an administrative than an instructional question.

In other ways internal class diversity has escaped attention. Both Barker Lunn (1970) and Daniels (1961), British writers interested in streaming, construe grouping within classes as a source of research design error, an obstacle to making clean comparisons between homogeneous and heterogeneous classes when the latter happen to employ grouping within the class. But by treating this phenomenon as error, they render it a nonproblem, at least in a substantive sense.

In one of the most important American studies, Borg (1965) explicitly indicates that ability grouping is often accompanied by different instructional treatments. In his own work he observes that a school district with classes distinguished by ability adjusts for differences among children by varying the rate of instruction. A contrasting district with heterogeneous classes adjusts instruction by enrichment. The distinction he draws between grouping and instruction is conceptually important; but once having made it, Borg ignores it empirically by failing to look for variations in rate or in enrichment *within* each school. As a result, the relation between within-class grouping and instruction does not arise as a problem.

Aside from the preoccupation in the study of grouping with the differences between homogeneous and heterogeneous groups, there has been a tendency for investigators to fixate on individual outcomes and experiences and to think about grouping simply as a way to cope with individual differences. We do not deny, of course, that individual out-·comes are important and that groups do influence individual experience. But to conceptualize grouping exclusively in individual terms ignores its organizational character and the sequential processes by which children are assigned to schools, to tracks, to grades, to classes, and within classes to groups. Each successive assignment raises different problems of how to deal with student diversity, for example, by territory at the school level and by age at the grade level. Children of the same age and in the same grade, moreover, differ by ability. And so the question arises of how the school manages grade-wide diversity so that instruction can be workable. Children can be assigned randomly or by some criterion such as ability. In either case, substantial diversity remains within classes, and one way or another teachers deal with it by using both organizational (like grouping) and instructional means.

In first grade, teachers characteristically employ ability groups for reading, but less characteristically do so for math. In both reading and math they must deal with class diversity—by using instruction geared to group differences or by using instructional variations adapted to whole class or seatwork formats. How well instruction is adapted to the whole class, to groups, or to individuals is an empirical question.

It is hard to understand why grouping inside classrooms has received as little attention as it has, especially because so much work, carried out as long ago as the 1930s (Burr 1931; Hartill 1936; West 1933) has shown persuasively that once grades are divided into homogeneously composed classes, substantial variation in ability remains in each class. How teachers deal with this diversity remains an intriguing issue. These early writers, it turns out, were not really interested in how schools or instruction worked, but rather tried to show that homogeneous grouping was not feasible because children grouped on one characteristic inevitably showed wide variations in others, and that in practice homogeneously grouped classes ended up overlapping in their distributions of ability. The difficulty for administrators in making defensible class assignments turned out to be the major agenda.

Our analysis of instructional grouping begins with the premise that grouping classes and instructing groups are entirely different things. The failure to draw the distinction has made it possible for partisans, for and against grouping, to praise it and condemn it. Ability groups, which are responses to characteristics of classes, we will argue, directly influence the design of instruction which in turn affects achievement. In modern elementary reading instruction carried out in primary classrooms, the abilities of students are treated as problematic and have given rise to the widespread use of instructional grouping. We pose a new question about ability grouping, one that is prompted by our broader formulation of schooling: How do the properties of a class influence the social arrangements that teachers design for reading instruction?

Organizing a class for instruction means transforming the initial distribution of some student characteristic, aptitude (or reading readiness) being the primary one. And as Kett's observations on nineteenth-century schools indicate, teachers also take such things as social maturity and obstreperousness into account because keeping the peace as well as providing instruction is part of their job. Teachers might take the class as it appears on the first day as given, as not problematic, and treat the individual aptitude distribution as an appropriate grouping arrangement for instruction. Four teachers in our study, in fact, took this course—at least for a while—by starting the year with whole class instruction. At the other extremes, teachers might create thirty "groups" in a class of thirty by individualizing instruction completely. Most teachers find these arrangements inappropriate for first grade reading although they do employ them for arithmetic.

The usual response of first grade teachers to the initial class distribution of aptitude is to transform it by creating an arrangement of groups that have aptitude distributions different from the whole class and that are smaller in size. The question before us now is whether the properties of the initial distribution influence the nature of the grouping arrangement into which it is transformed. And if there is a connection between these two properties of classes—aptitude distribution and grouping arrangement—what is the nature of it? Consider some possibilities.

Class distributions of aptitude come in different shapes—concentrated, spread out, bimodal, asymmetrical—and grouping arrangements are constrained by these distributional properties. Given two classes, one dispersed and the other concentrated, the groups in the former will be spread out. Obviously, classes composed of abler children may not need as much intensively supervised instruction as classes composed of their less able counterparts. The former can learn more on their own, require less help, and thus prosper in large groups; their slower colleagues in contrast may need the close watching and support that smaller groups make possible. But if there are many low readiness children, one small group may not accommodate them. Two groups may be needed or perhaps one large one. Yet, teachers rarely start the year with more than three groups. If two are already used up accommodating a large contingent of low aptitude children, will one suffice for the remainder? Perhaps, if the remainder is not itself too diverse. But if two are needed for the remainder, will not a very large low aptitude group be difficult to teach, maybe almost as hard as the whole class? In short, the grouping arrangement, given the class distribution, is not cut from whole cloth.

Grouping is a scheme for organizing a class for instruction, not for instructing it. (Instruction, as we explain later in chapter 5, is a group phenomenon even when it involves all the children in the class at once.) We proceed now to an empirical investigation of how alternative grouping arrangements are shaped by the aptitude distribution of classes. In turn, we show how those initial arrangements become modified when they prove to be instructionally problematic to teachers over the course of the school year.

CLASS DISTRIBUTIONS AND GROUPING CONFIGURATIONS

The Distributional Properties of Classes

We have argued that the most basic condition (although not the sole one) that teachers contemplate as they establish a program of instruction is the distribution of children's aptitudes; and because we are interested in reading, reading aptitude (or readiness) is most germane. This is so because teachers must find ways to adapt their talents, time, and resources to what children can do and to changes in what they can do if instruction is to be viable, and aptitude is an appropriate indication of such capacity.

Several aspects of the class aptitude distribution are relevant to the establishment of groups and their subsequent instruction. The first of these recognizes that aptitudes are dispersed more or less widely throughout the class. When children's aptitudes are widely dispersed, teachers will be pressed to make provisions for wider differences in instructional needs than they will if all children are just about the same. The standard deviation of class aptitude provides an indication of conditions requiring more or less diversified instructional approaches. Obviously, to identify a requirement does not mean it will actually be met; and some teachers do provide the same instruction for all children irrespective of their differences.

The second aspect recognizes that independently of aptitude dispersion, teachers confront conditions of distributional imbalance, that is, the presence of clusters of children with special needs at the top or bottom of a class. The skewness of aptitude, then, measures whether the distribution requires that the teacher attend to special interests and needs located asymmetrically in the class. It is a commonplace of teaching that aside from disruptive children, the ones who learn slowly for whatever reason are difficult to deal with.

The third aspect, the number of low aptitude children, superficially resembles positive skewness and represents a particular kind of instructional burden, the presence of large numbers of children likely to experience difficulty and to require substantial teacher attention whether the class is asymmetrically distributed or not. We maintain that the number and not the proportion is the better index; the more there are, the heavier the burden, and a small proportion in a very large class can represent a substantial number and create considerable difficulty for the teacher. By implication, a large contingent of high aptitude children is not so problematic. Able children can turn their brightness into ingenious disruption, but by and large, and with a modicum of planning, it is not too difficult to give bright children their heads because their basic mastery of the material is not usually in question.

Fourth, we consider the size of the class, for if classes are large, one or more of the groups is likely to be large. For some purposes and under some conditions, a large group is an instructional advantage while under others it is a liability.

An observant reader will have noticed, first, that two of the properties of class distributions pertinent to the formation of groups happen to be the familiar statistical moments and, second, that the first moment and the most familiar one—the mean—is missing. Standard deviation, skewness, and size all pertain in different ways to the spread of the distribution, to its diversity, which is what we believe teachers attend to as they form groups. The mean, however, denotes central tendency and theoretically should not help us understand the formation of groups, which are solutions to problems of diversity. Under conditions of whole class teaching, for example, knowing the mean might tell something about where teachers pitch the difficulty of instruction; that is, if all children in a class are slow learners, a teacher would not be likely to use advanced materials or to run through them quickly. (We will show in the next chapter that the mean aptitude of groups rather than of classes is indeed a major condition influencing the design of instruction.) But mean aptitude of the class does not tell us what is problematic for the teacher as far as group formation is concerned. Nevertheless, as we indicated in chapter 2, studies of educational effects frequently employ measures of school or class climate based upon the mean. Thus, for practical reasons pertaining to the current state of knowledge and to the contention of some investigators that the class mean really does have instructional importance, we include it; though from the perspective of our argument, its utility for understanding group formation is doubtful.

These five properties were determined for the fifteen classes in our sample in the following manner. Size was reported by teachers. Estimates of the aptitude distribution were based on the random sample of children drawn from each class, as described in chapter 3. Class means, standard deviations, and skewness were calculated using conventional procedures. The number of low aptitude children was determined by the number in each class sample scoring below 25 on the Word Learning Tasks (approximately 30 percent of the total sample; see appendix D for the distribution of aptitude).

(We must note parenthetically that these same distributional indices are relevant to other levels of school system organization—district, school, and instructional group—and that in each case their meaning differs depending on the organizational agenda of these other levels.)

Group Formation

When teachers establish reading groups, they transform the aptitude composition of the class; for that reason, we must keep in mind the distinction between the properties of groups and those of classes. The reason for reorganizing a class is to make it easier to manage, to make it easier to teach, and/or to make instruction more effective (or apparently so). According to the conventional wisdom, the standard way to do all these things is to teach aggregations of children that are smaller than whole classes. Once teachers reach this conclusion, the alternatives before them become not only limited in number but collectively constraining.

First, teachers must determine the *number* of instructional groups. The class as a whole might be treated as an instructional unit (uncommon for reading, but common for math) or else divided into groups. But into how many? The number will be constrained by the size of the class but, more importantly, by practical considerations related to the number of distinct preparations the teacher must make and to the difficulty of supervising the large class remainder left over when the teacher is instructing a small group. The more groups, the smaller the size of each and the larger the remainder. One rarely finds as many as five or six reading groups. Experience and tradition characteristically limit the number established at the beginning of the year to three, sometimes two or four.

Having determined the number of groups, a teacher must decide upon *relative group size.* Groups may all be equal, or some may be large while others are small. We expect that such varied considerations as the management capabilities of the teacher and the number of books available may constrain the maximum size of groups. But in keeping with our presumption that children with low aptitude are hard to teach, we expect that if teachers form groups of unequal size, the one composed of low aptitude children will be smaller than those with abler children. But that may depend on how many low aptitude children there are; for if there are many, a small group may not accommodate them all.

Finally, teachers can vary the *discreteness* of groups, the extent to which aptitudes do not overlap group boundaries. In a class of two groups, for example, the low group may be composed of children only from the lower end of the aptitude range and the high group only from the upper end. In a class with completely overlapping groups, by contrast, each one reflects the distributive properties of the class—a case of heterogeneous grouping in which only the size of instructional units but not the distribution of the class is transformed. Teachers who want to work with groups smaller in size than the whole class, but who are not overly concerned about decreasing its diversity, will not form discrete groups. Most teachers, we expect, form groups that overlap, partially because children's characteristics other than aptitude, such as work skills and motivation, are taken into account. Furthermore, aptitude might be difficult to assess accurately in a collective setting particularly at the beginning of the first grade.

The alternatives available to teachers in forming groups—the number of groups formed, whether they are of equal or unequal size, and their discreteness—characterize the group configuration of classes. Classes, then, may be described not only by their distributive properties, but also by the configuration of groups composing them. The configurational properties assume particular importance because of their implications for the design of instruction.

The number of groups is important because it affects the proportion of time a teacher can allocate to their direct and intensive supervision and to the relatively unsupervised seatwork undertaken by the remainder of the class. For example, in classes meeting for the same length of time, one with two groups has equal amounts of time allocated to seatwork and supervised small group instruction while one with four groups has three times as much allocated to seatwork as to small group instruction. Groups b, c, and d must simply wait their turns doing seatwork while the teacher is busy with group a. The number of groups, then, influences the trade-off between direct instruction and seatwork.

The relative size of groups in a class can be important for instruction, particularly if the small group contains children of low aptitude. It should be easier to provide appropriate instruction for fewer than for more such children because each child has a greater opportunity to participate in instruction and to receive support and guidance. Although small group size might also enhance the learning of brighter children, they are better able to cope with less optimal conditions. For that reason, we would not expect to find much benefit from smaller group size among learners of average or higher ability.

Although the discreteness of groups has only indirect implications for instructional design, it bears directly on how much groups differ from each other in average ability, as indicated by the range of group means. Teachers do not differentiate instruction much in overlapping groups that by definition do not differ greatly in composition. By contrast, discrete groups differ more in mean aptitude and perforce in the instruction designed for them. The range of group means, influenced by discreteness, provides an estimate of how varied the instruction of groups within a class is expected to be. As a class characteristic, the range bears a direct relation to a group level property: namely, the group mean aptitude, which we argue in the next chapter is the main characteristic toward which teachers gear their instruction.

We have discussed here two orders of class properties: first, characteristics of the aptitude distribution; second, aspects of classroom grouping arrangements. The former order is straightforward, the latter more complex. We have indicated that the grouping arrangements of *classes* differ in the number of groups formed; in whether the groups are of equal or unequal sizes; and in the extent to which they overlap in aptitude, which influences the range of group means. Most importantly, these are not group designations but class properties defined by the configuration of groups composing the class.

To calculate these indices of grouping configuration, we first estimated the size and distributive properties of groups within classes. The group membership of each child in the sample was determined by asking first grade teachers to report the group in which each was instructed in December and May of first grade. From this information, we estimated the size and aptitude characteristics of instructional groups. For example, as shown in table 4.1, seventeen out of thirty-seven children in class 01 were studied. Four of these were in the low group, six in the middle group, and seven in the high group. These numbers constitute the random samples from which the actual group sizes were estimated; nine, thirteen, and fifteen, respectively, and similarly for groups in the other classes (appendix B contains sample and estimated group characteristics for the fall). Whereas the sample sizes provide good estimates of group size and mean aptitude, they are too small in some cases to yield reliable indices of other distributive properties (the higher statistical moments). Nevertheless, estimates of group variation were used in aggregated form to determine the degree of discreteness in the composition of groups.

The calculation of the indices of group configuration is shown in appendix E. The number of groups in classes ranged from one to four. The Size Inequality Index ranged from 0.00 to 10.00, with low values indicating classes with groups of nearly equal size. Values for the Discreteness Index ranged from -0.46 to 1.00. (See appendix E for an explanation of the anomalous negative values of this index.) The range in values from 0.65 to 1.00 refers to instructional groups that tend toward discreteness, while the range from 0.20 to 0.64 indicates moderate degrees of overlap. Low values, especially the negative ones, indicate high overlap among groups. And as for Group Range, the differences in mean aptitude between the highest and lowest groups in the classes varied from 12.00 to 51.33 for December grouping patterns.

Linkages between Class Distributions

We can now rephrase our question about the influence of class properties on grouping patterns in precise terms: How do the size and distributive properties of classes influence the number of groups formed by teachers, their relative size, their discreteness, and their range in mean aptitude?

What conditions influence a teacher to form more rather than fewer instructional groups? Three class properties are plausible candidates. The first is the size of the class. In first grade reading, it is easier to plan instruction for and manage smaller rather than larger groups. In classes with the same number of groups, the larger the class, the larger the groups within it. If smaller groups are desired, larger classes will contain more groups on the average than smaller ones.

Second, over and above class size, diversity will lead to more groups if teachers try to increase group homogeneity.

Finally, more groups will be formed when a class contains a large contingent of low aptitude children in order to accommodate better their instructional needs.

What class properties might lead a teacher to form groups of unequal size? As previously suggested, small groups are likely to be established to accommodate low aptitude children. Yet the shape of the class distribution should influence whether small groups will be feasible. To help think about this issue, visualize several class distributions including a positively skewed class containing a predominance of low aptitude children, a negatively skewed class with many able children, and a normally distributed class. In normal (symmetrical) and negatively skewed classes, creating a small group can markedly decrease the heterogeneity of the low end of the distribution. It can have only a minor effect in decreasing heterogeneity in positively skewed classes because the low aptitude children are numerous and thickly bunched together; hence creating a small group does little to decrease the existing narrow variation at the bottom of the class. In the negatively skewed class, the spread over the lower tail of the distribution is very wide; a small group narrows the diversity more than a large one does; and while the remaining diversity is still large, it can be managed in a group of small size. We therefore expect to find unequal sized groups in classes *not* burdened by a large number of low aptitude children because in this situation the small low group provides the remedies of small size and homogeneity.

In classes containing many such children, a small low group does not help the teacher manage the whole low aptitude burden. It will accommodate a portion of it, but a substantial low aptitude contingent will remain. In effect, the crowded bottom of the class is already homogeneous and numerous, and a small low group fails to relieve the problem of numbers and forces the creation of highly diverse groups farther up the scale. Small low groups are only advantageous at the bottom when the class is normally distributed or negatively skewed—conditions with only a few low aptitude children to begin with.

We suspect that the overlap among groups may arise only in part by design. It may partly be a function of the difficulty teachers face in accurately assessing aptitude; it may also occur, not as a response to class properties, but from teacher preferences for similar groups that equalize the instructional experience of their members. In homogeneous classes, aptitude differences are less distinct and the same instruction may be appropriate for many children; hence, whether or not the groups overlap much may not matter. The opposite is true for diverse classes, which are likely to be characterized by discrete groups and highly differentiated instruction to accommodate the range of aptitude differences.

The range among groups in mean aptitude should directly reflect class diversity. Classes composed of students differing widely in aptitude (large class standard deviation) should then on the average yield groups characterized by very different means. Nevertheless, the degree to which groups are distinct in composition also has a bearing. One can imagine a highly diverse class divided into two completely overlapping instructional groups with little difference between them in mean aptitude. Our argument, however, is that diversity supports the creation of groups that overlap relatively little with the result that the groups differ markedly in mean aptitude. We turn now to the empirical examination of group formation.

INITIAL GROUPING

Class Properties

Table 4.1 shows that the fifteen first grade classes differ considerably in size, with the smallest in school C and the largest in schools A, B, and F. Classes also differ in their distributional properties. Mean aptitude varies within schools as well as among them, with the greatest range of class means appearing in school F. Only a few classes are narrowly dispersed, and these tend to be relatively low in average aptitude as well (classes 02, 04, 06, and 15).

Clear differences exist in skewness, particularly in school F where classes reflect a modified grade-wide pattern of ability grouping for reading instruction. Class 13 contains a large cohort of the most able children in the grade along with a small contingent of the least able. Class 14 includes the next ablest segment of the grade distribution with another small group with low aptitude, and class 15 contains the low-middle range of the grade. This special form of ability grouping helps to account for the unusual combination of distributive properties found in school F classes.

Classes differ markedly in the number of low aptitude children. To some extent the number reflects total class size; obviously, larger classes might be expected on average to include a greater number of less able children. However, the proportion, as well as the absolute number, is higher, more so in the classes of schools A, B, and D than in the others. In keeping with our assumption that low aptitude children represent a heavy instructional burden, we view these classes as potentially more problematic than those with fewer. If grouping configurations are responsive to the character of classes, we would expect to see different

TABLE 4.1
DISTRIBUTIONAL PROPERTIES OF CLASSES

District	School	Class	Actual Size	Sample Size	Children's Aptitude			Number of Low Aptitude Children	Number of Groups	
					Mean	Standard Deviation	Skewness		Fall	Spring
I	A	01	37	17	40.47	21.34	−0.06	11	3	3
	B	02	35	13	25.54	10.13	0.99	19	3	4
		03	36	18	36.94	17.03	0.49	8	3	4
		04	30	6	32.50	14.61	0.51	10	2[a]	2
		05	35	8	29.50	18.59	1.53	22	3	3
II	C	06	20	6	34.00	11.85	0.32	3	2	2
		07	20	6	46.17	20.18	0.25	3	1	2
		08	19	7	43.43	16.21	0.73	0	1	2
	D	09	27	12	35.92	20.24	0.75	9	3	3
		10	27	8	37.63	26.85	0.63	17	3	4
III	E	11	28	7	38.29	18.40	0.74	4	3	4
		12	29	9	40.89	20.73	0.48	6	2	3
	F	13	37	8	53.38	21.08	−1.16	9	2	2
		14	33	14	44.14	18.76	−0.10	7	3	3
		15	36	8	31.63	13.14	0.98	14	1	2

[a] These are two first grade groups. Class 04 also had one group of second graders.

grouping arrangements in classes containing many rather than few low aptitude children.

Class Properties and Number of Groups

Table 4.1 also shows that teachers differ in the number of groups they form in the fall, from one to three. Most have three groups (classes 01, 02, 03, 05, 09, 10, 11, and 14), while some employ total class instruction (classes 07, 08, and 15) or establish two groups (classes 04, 06, 12, and 13). Table 4.2 shows that class size and the number of low aptitude children are moderately related to the number of groups, approaching but not achieving statistical significance.

By contrast, class mean, standard deviation, and skewness of aptitude are much less strongly related to the number of groups formed. We did not expect the mean or skewness to be associated with the number of groups; but if groups do perform the function of reducing class diversity, it is reasonable to expect more groups in highly diverse classes. However, we find no such relation. On the basis of these findings we suggest that the sheer number of children in a class more than their dispersion influences the forming of a workable grouping arrangement for first grade reading instruction. However, class differences in aptitude are important, but at the lower end of the aptitude distribution. That is, the number of groups formed reflects more the numbers of children in the lower end of the aptitude distribution than the total spread of aptitude, the mean class level, and skewness.

TABLE 4.2
CORRELATION COEFFICIENTS BETWEEN
CLASS DISTRIBUTIONAL PROPERTIES AND
THE NUMBER OF INSTRUCTIONAL GROUPS
FORMED IN DECEMBER (n = 15)

Class Distributional Properties	Correlation Coefficients
Class Size	0.46
Children's Aptitude	
Mean	−0.28
Standard Deviation	0.25
Skewness	0.09
Number of Low Aptitude Children	0.46

Levels of significance: 0.05: r > 0.50.

Grouping Types

The characterization of grouping arrangements by the number of groups formed, although perhaps representing the most significant feature of the grouping pattern, fails to capture the different ways in which arrangements are employed. All classes with three groups—low, middle, and high—represent a conventional form of aptitude grouping. Less conventional arrangements are found in the three classes of school C, two of the three classes in school F, and classes 04 and 12.

In school C, two classes are not subdivided, while the third is divided into two equal groups. Does this represent two different patterns within the same school? We think not. Our data portray the grouping pattern found in December; but we know from interviews that class 06 had one group of twenty children only a few weeks before the data were collected, and that classes 07 and 08 were going to split early in January. (Spring data indicate that they did.) Thus, we find all classes in school C beginning the year with whole class instruction, then splitting in the late fall or early winter into two groups. Only the timing of the split distinguishes the three. Thus, class size appears to have direct consequences for the number of groups established, and also seems to influence whether grouping occurs at the beginning of the year or is delayed.

In school F, instructional groups vary in number. The two classes of able children with a few less able ones are grouped along aptitude lines. The third class (15), to which middle aptitude children were assigned, operates as a single instructional group. It is clear that the special distributional properties of these classes affect the number and size of instructional groups.

The remaining schools follow a traditional arrangement. Even class 12 appears to be similar in organization; while only two groups are established initially, three are used by spring. Class 04 is an exceptional case—a split grade 1 and 2 class. Fifteen of the thirty class members were first graders, and the teacher grouped them into two groups (we have assumed that one group was used for the second graders, for a total of three groups). The teacher, experiencing her first year on the job, attempted to group the first graders on the basis of ability and therefore is properly classified with the other teachers in school B as following a traditional grouping arrangement.

In sum, represented in our sample are three distinct types of grouping. School C classes are characterized by delayed grouping and class patterns consisting of no more than two groups (delayed grouping). School F classes employ a modified ability grouping of the whole first grade into classes, followed by instructional grouping within classes (grade-wide grouping). Finally, the classes in the remaining schools reflect patterns of traditional ability grouping (traditional grouping).

TABLE 4.3
ANALYSIS OF VARIANCE OF CLASS DISTRIBUTIONAL PROPERTIES: CHILDREN'S APTITUDES BY GROUPING TYPE

Class Distributional Properties	Means of Group Types			Grand Mean	F Ratio	Significance Level
	Delayed (C)	Grade-wide (F)	Traditional (A,B,D,E)			
Class Size	19.67	35.33	31.56	29.93	17.62	0.00**
Children's Aptitude						
Mean	41.20	43.05	35.30	38.03	1.95	0.18
Standard Dev.	16.08	17.66	18.66	17.94	0.38	0.69
Skewness	0.43	−0.09	0.67	0.47	2.04	0.17
Number of Low Aptitude Children	2.00	10.00	11.78	9.47	3.87	0.0506[a]
Number of Classes	3	3	9	15		

* $p < 0.05$. ** $p < 0.01$.   [a] Closely approaches significance.

Table 4.3 shows the findings from the previous correlational analysis presented as an analysis of variance comparing the three types of grouping according to their class properties. The three are not distinguished by the mean, standard deviation, or skewness of class aptitude. Only class size and the number of low aptitude children distinguish the delayed grouping type from the others.

The correlation between class size and grouping type suggests that teachers of small classes may initially avoid ability grouping, while teachers of large classes may be constrained to group from the beginning of the school year. Perhaps teachers of small classes find it possible to give children who experience difficulty sufficient support without creating a separate group for them.

In any event, this analysis provides evidence supporting the relation between class size and type of grouping pattern. But while the number of low aptitude children in school C classes is considerably smaller than that in most of the other classes, school E classes have a limited number of low aptitude children but still employ traditional grouping. This suggests that a small number of low aptitude children does not necessarily lead to delayed grouping. The proper interpretation of the findings is probably that unusual forms, such as delayed grouping, may only be feasible when optimal conditions of classes—such as small size and few low aptitude children—prevail. In short, teachers can exercise options, but which ones they take will depend on the congeniality of other conditions.

We turn now to more detailed analysis of the relations between class properties and grouping arrangements. We consider the three types of grouping separately, beginning with the classes in schools C and F, and then turning to the traditionally grouped classes, treating them as exemplary case studies.

Delayed grouping. The three teachers in school C began the year with total class instruction. Class 06, the first to be divided into groups, can be distinguished from classes 07 and 08 by its lower mean and standard deviation, but not by its skewness, or number of low aptitude children. As table 4.4 shows, classes 06 and 07 are divided on the basis of ability as indicated by the moderate to high indices of discreteness. By contrast, the discreteness coefficient of 0.00 for class 08 indicates that groups are not formed on the basis of ability; instead each reflects the distributional properties of the class. As a result, the range of group means is considerably smaller in class 08 than in the other two classes—this in spite of the greater variation (standard deviation) among class members in class 08 than in class 06 (shown in table 4.1).

In addition to using only two groups, teachers in school C form groups of equal or nearly equal size as indicated by the inequality index. From arguments made earlier, we would not expect equal sized groups for such normal class distributions. It appears that the grouping arrange-ments in school C are governed by the preferences of teachers and made possible by favorable class properties (small size, few low aptitude chil-dren). Interviews with teachers in school C indicated that they tried to equalize the learning experiences of children as much as possible out of concern that children would make invidious comparisons among them-selves related to group placement. The initial employment of whole class instruction conforms to their preference for the equalization of experi-ence. However, in two of the three classes, once grouping occurred, it was based on aptitude. Only teacher 08's groups appear to decrease group size without decreasing aptitude dispersion—a case of hetero-geneous grouping. When grouping does appear in the late fall and early winter, it takes an unusual form: two large instructional groups rather than the more customary three.

We also note, however, that the three classes have standard deviations comparably as large as those found in the other schools, indicating that the teachers had to confront the problem of diversity in the distribution of aptitude. Not surprisingly, they created instructional groups.

Those who believe in ability grouping would find sufficient variation in school C classes to create groups. Those objecting to it, like teachers 06, 07, and 08, find opportunities first to delay grouping and then to institute a pattern that represents concessions both to the reality of a diverse aptitude distribution and to their preference for the equalization of children's experiences.

Grade-wide grouping. Teachers regrouped the first graders in school F for reading instruction into two bimodally distributed classes and one containing the low-middle range in aptitude. As might be expected on the basis of its distribution, class 13 was divided into two instructional groups corresponding to its patently bimodal concentrations of chil-dren—a very large high and a very small low group. Its index of dis-creteness is therefore extremely high and the groups are characterized by widely separated means as shown in table 4.4. The size inequality index is also high.

Class 14 has a similar bimodal distribution, although the children are slightly less able. The teacher, like teacher 13, formed groups of unequal size, but with one large high group and two very small lower groups. While this arrangement of groups fits the class distribution, one would not necessarily expect to find high overlap in aptitude as indicated by the low index of discreteness (table 4.4); yet an inspection of individual placements reveals that some low aptitude children are placed in the high group. For this reason, the means of the groups are more alike than would be expected on the basis of the distributional properties of the class. The high group, because of its wide aptitude dispersion, would not appear to be viable, and indeed, we find that in the spring of the

TABLE 4.4
CONFIGURATIONAL PROPERTIES OF CLASSES IN SCHOOLS C AND F, FALL AND SPRING

School	Class	Fall				Spring			
		Number of Groups	Size Inequality	Discreteness	Range of Group Means	Number of Groups	Size Inequality	Discreteness	Range of Group Means
C	06	2	0.00	0.50	15.34	2	0.00	0.50	15.34
	07	1	—	—	—	2	0.00	0.74	31.00
	08	1	—	—	—	2	1.50	0.00	6.25
F	13	2	9.50	0.98	43.83	2	9.50	0.98	45.33
	14	3	10.00	0.00	29.18	3	5.33	0.13	33.20
	15	1	—	—	—	2	8.00	0.00	3.75

year some of the low aptitude members of the high group are transferred to another group. (Group change and transfer are discussed in greater detail later in the chapter.)

Class 15, characterized by the lowest mean and the smallest standard deviation, includes children spanning the middle aptitude range of the grade. Teaching this class as a single group is not expected to be workable because of the large number of low readiness children; not surprisingly, two groups are formed later in the year, suggesting that instructional problems resulted from treating the class as a single group.

The teachers in school F use a modified aptitude grouping plan. Its use is not predictable on the basis of the school's distributional properties and therefore must be attributed to administrator and/or teacher preferences because there are obviously alternative ways to accommodate a similar grade-wide composition. Nevertheless, once classes are established, the number and relative size of their groups are predictable with the exception of class 15, where two initial groups might have been expected rather than one.

Traditional grouping. All classes using traditional grouping (01, 02, 03, 04, 05, 09, 10, 11, and 12) are large. They differ considerably, however, in mean aptitude, standard deviation, skewness, and number of low aptitude children, as table 4.1 shows. While teacher preferences unrelated to class distributional properties might account for the early employment of conventional grouping, compared to its delayed use in school C classes, class size stands out as the single most important and plausible determinant of early grouping. Large classes evidently pose problems of management; so does a large contingent of low aptitude children. Grouping is a workable arrangement for both eventualities.

Given traditional grouping, do the distributional properties of the class influence grouping arrangements? With respect to the number of groups, only in class 12 did the teacher divide children into two groups; in all other classes, a three-group autumn pattern was used. Accordingly, there is insufficient variation in the sample to test the influence of class size on the number of groups.

Earlier we speculated that the use of small low groups might occur in normally distributed classes but not in those containing large numbers of low aptitude children. Our nine classes cluster into two groups: those with many low aptitude children (02, 05, and 10) and those with few (01, 03, 04, 09, 11, and 12), as shown in table 4.1. To appreciate the magnitude of the burden in the first three classes, notice that the low aptitude children constitute from 54 to 63 percent of total class enrollment.

The three classes containing very large numbers of such children are characterized by equal sized groups as indicated by the low inequality index reported in table 4.5. Only one other class, 12, is characterized by an inequality index under 2.0. We have no explanation why a teacher with a normally distributed class might form equal sized groups. Except for class 12, classes with fewer low aptitude children contain groups of unequal size. Further, in every case, the smallest group is composed of low aptitude children. This preliminary analysis indicates, then, that the relative size of groups is related to the number of low aptitude children in the class.

We argued that the discreteness of groups reflects the aptitude dispersion of a class. Four are characterized by high standard deviations: 01, 09, 10, and 12. Their discreteness scores range from 0.65 to 1.00, indicating highly discrete groups. Table 4.5 shows that all four classes with high standard deviations also contain groups that did not overlap much. The teacher of a fifth class, 05, also formed highly discrete groups even though her class was only moderately dispersed (st. dev. = 18.59). Generally, it appears that teachers group highly varied classes into more discrete groups than is true for less dispersed classes; however, discrete grouping can appear in less varied classes, as illustrated by the pattern of teacher 05.

The dispersion of the class is also manifested in the aptitude range between top and bottom groups as shown by three of the four dispersed classes characterized by a wide range of group means; class 09 represents the exception. Class 05 is also characterized by a wide range of group means even though its dispersion falls in the moderate range. This case demonstrates that the degree to which groups overlap directly influences the range of group means. Reciprocally, even in a highly varied class, a teacher who forms highly overlapping groups can diminish the differences among groups. Class 09 is characterized by a borderline discreteness score (0.65), and this may account for the narrower range of group means than expected on the basis of class dispersion.

To test more systematically the relation between class and grouping properties for traditional grouping, zero-order coefficients were calculated as shown in table 4.6. The correlational results generally confirm the prior observations. The number of low aptitude children is related to the relative size of instructional groups at a statistically significant level; no other class properties are associated with size inequality. The standard deviation of classes bears a substantial, but nonsignificant relation to the discreteness of groups and a statistically significant correlation with the range of group means. No other class properties bear a substantial association with discreteness or range of group means.

Two observations about grouping need emphasis. The first pertains to the relative size of groups and the second to the nature of overlap among them. In almost every case where a relatively small group appears in a class, it is composed of low aptitude children. This means that the size inequality index reflects the smaller size of low groups. The relative

TABLE 4.5
CONFIGURATIONAL PROPERTIES OF CLASSES IN SCHOOLS A, B, D, AND E, FALL AND SPRING

School	Class	Fall				Spring			
		Number of Groups	Size Inequality	Discreteness	Range of Group Means	Number of Groups	Size Inequality	Discreteness	Range of Group Means
A	01	3	2.23	0.75	41.21	3	7.77	0.64	32.32
B	02	3	0.90	0.17	12.00	4	2.25	0.02	14.50
	03	3	5.33	0.64	34.39	4	3.00	0.52	36.36
	04	2	5.00	0.23	15.75	2	5.00	0.01	12.75
	05	3	1.77	0.83	40.17	3	1.78	0.40	28.67
D	09	3	4.67	0.65	31.17	3	8.00	0.07	21.00
	10	3	1.33	1.00	51.33	4	1.88	1.00	54.00
E	11	3	4.44	-0.46	21.50	4	1.50	0.49	35.50
	12	2	1.50	0.93	37.46	3	2.44	0.75	44.75

size of groups is not determined solely by the distribution of class aptitude; it may also reflect teacher preference for a small low group, when the distributional character of a class permits, because of the greater ease in dealing with low aptitude children in smaller groups.

Among those teachers who composed groups that overlapped in aptitude, two major types of arrangement were observed. The first involved the formation of two groups composed of children from the same portion of the class distribution. For example, teacher 10 formed two highly overlapping groups at the lower end of the class. This pattern suggests that she saw these children as sufficiently alike to profit from the same instructional program, but still created two groups in order to reduce group size, most likely to manage them more easily. Fewer children per group allow the teacher more time to interact with each and to identify and remedy the problems each one encounters during instruction.

The second type of overlap involves placing low aptitude children in middle and high groups. High aptitude children are never placed in low groups. Groups in classes 11 and 14, and to a lesser extent in class 02, are characterized by this sort of overlap. How can we understand it? One possible explanation is that some teachers have difficulty assessing children's aptitudes accurately, especially low aptitudes. Alternatively, they may consider other characteristics than aptitude in forming groups. For example, we can imagine placing children with good work habits and social adjustment in a higher group than expected simply on the basis of aptitude.

Three major conclusions can be drawn from this examination of the relations between class conditions and group patterns. First, class size is a determinant of the number of groups. However, this relation appears to be mediated by the type of grouping scheme teachers use. Further, the nature of the relation is conditional. While small class size permits teachers to group pupils according to preference, large class size is associated with traditional patterns of ability grouping.

TABLE 4.6

CORRELATION COEFFICIENTS BETWEEN CLASS DISTRIBUTIONAL PROPERTIES AND INDICES OF GROUP CONFIGURATION IN SCHOOL A, B, D, AND E CLASSES (n = 9)

Class Distributional Properties	Number of Groups	Size Inequality	Discreteness	Range of Group Means
Class Size	0.28	−0.16	0.11	0.05
Children's Aptitudes				
Mean	−0.15	0.20	0.22	0.54
Standard Deviation	0.12	−0.16	0.56	0.89**
Skewness	0.23	−0.21	−0.09	−0.14
Number of Low Aptitude				
Children	0.35	−0.62*	0.35	0.18

* p < 0.05.   ** p < 0.01.

Second, the dispersion of a class is closely related both to the degree of discreteness among groups and to the aptitude range of group means. Further, discreteness and the range of group means are conditionally linked so that an increase in overlap among groups decreases the range of group means in a class. Generally, however, most grouping is based on pupil aptitude, and the aptitude of most children, particularly those in the middle and high portions of the distribution, seems to be accurately assessed.

Finally, a large concentration of pupils in the lower end of the class distribution is associated with equal sized groups. By contrast, teachers of more normally distributed classes have the option of forming either equal sized groups (which means a large low group) or a relatively small low group. Again, we see a conditional relation of a special sort: a more optimally composed class permits teachers to exercise their preferences, while less optimal conditions constrain teachers toward a single solution.

We have gained some understanding of the determinants of initial grouping patterns. An important further question is whether the initial grouping scheme remains satisfactory beyond the beginning of the year, and this question leads us to examine patterns of group change and of individual change between groups.

Changes in Grouping from Fall to Spring

The description of fall class and instructional group characteristics provides a sense of how teachers initially organize classes to cope with the distribution of children's aptitudes. They begin the school year with little to go on in establishing a basis for group organization. Our evidence indicates that they take certain class characteristics into account, but that group formation in its particular manifestations is not determined in any direct way by the distribution of class characteristics.

Groups established during the fall of the school year are by no means static; they change over time as does their membership. They change in number, in size, and in membership to the extent that they gain members from and lose them to other groups. School and class size and their distributional properties did not change in our sample from fall to spring; accordingly, the changes we observe pertain only to instructional groups.

When new groups are added and change in size, children must obviously have been transferred from one to another. Nevertheless, group change must not be construed solely as the transfer of individual children. While it has an important individual component, both group and class considerations are also involved. Groups or classes having certain properties may have a greater susceptibility to change than others with different properties. Thus, individuals transfer; and groups form and split. Transferring individuals may enter existing groups, possibly changing the latter's size and composition, or they may constitute a new group. Accordingly, to understand individual transfers, we look at the characteristics of individuals; to understand group change, we look at properties of classes and groups.

Individual Transfers between Instructional Groups

The analysis of individual change pertains to classes in all schools except C because the latter's classes have properties that make an analysis of individual transfers inappropriate. As indicated earlier, classes in school C all started the year with whole class instruction, a pattern that yielded, between late fall and early winter, to grouped instruction with only two groups in each class. In our judgment, it would be incorrect to treat the division of those three classes as involving the transfer of individual children. Rather, each class was divided. Once established, the group membership remained stable. Moreover, we suspect that transferring children between groups would have been contrary to teacher preferences, indicating by implication that the groups were different and that children would get an instructional experience in one group that was unavailable in another.

Table 4.7 shows the percentage of children in each class of schools A, B, D, E, and F who remained in their initial group or changed from one to another. Based upon the number of sampled children (n = 128), the table shows aggregate patterns of transfer (class specific): the percentage of the children who remain in their original group, who move upward, and who move downward. Note that in school F, some children transfer between groups within their original class while others transfer by moving to another class.

On the whole, more children remain in their original fall group for the whole year (about 70 percent) than change although there is substantial variation by school and by class. Three classes show an extremely high percentage of children changing groups: classes 04, 11, and 14. (It is difficult to draw conclusions about class 04 because of its split grade composition.) Note, however, that the other two classes are characterized by extremely high overlap caused by the placement of low aptitude children in middle and high groups. We suspect that whatever the reason for this overlap, it leads to groups that are difficult to instruct, and that the high rate of change represents the efforts of the teacher to form groups that are easier to deal with.

As table 4.7 shows, about equal proportions of children move to higher and to lower groups. However, classes differ in the relative proportion of upward versus downward movement. Four classes contain large proportions of children moving upward: 01, 03, 09, and 11. None of these was distinguished by many low aptitude children. This tendency will be explored later when we discuss group changes.

TABLE 4.7
PERCENTAGE OF CHILDREN IN EACH CLASS REMAINING IN
THE SAME INSTRUCTIONAL GROUP AND CHANGING GROUPS

School	Class	No Change	Change Upward	Downward
A	01	75.68	24.32	0.00
B	02	77.15	14.28	8.57
	03	66.67	22.22	11.11
	04	33.33	16.67	50.00
	05	88.57	11.43	0.00
D	09	74.07	25.93	0.00
	10	77.78	11.11	11.11
E	11	42.85	42.85	14.30
	12	65.52	10.34	24.14
F	13	86.49	0.00	0.00
		13.51[a]	0.00[a]	0.00[a]
	14	36.36	0.00	36.36
		6.06[a]	0.00[a]	21.21[a]
	15	88.89	0.00	11.11
Total		70.51	14.36	15.13

Note: Data in this table exclude school C.   [a] These figures
indicate children who change classes.

To determine what considerations teachers keep in mind when making such changes, we are concerned with two characteristics of children
who changed groups: aptitude and learning. Do teachers take aptitude
into account as the basis for changing a child's group, or do they consider
how much the child has learned? Of the children who moved upward
from their original group, 55.4 percent were above their group's mean
in aptitude; of the children who moved downward, 57.6 percent were
below their group's mean in aptitude. In short, there is a rather weak
relation between relative aptitude score and the likelihood of children
transferring between groups.

Although aptitude might serve as the basis for transfer out of initial
fall groups, we expected that the actual learning of material would provide a better explanation of the children who transferred upward. Sev-
enty-five percent were above the mean of their fall group in the number
of words learned by December; and of those who moved downward,
73.9 percent were below the mean of their fall group in the number of
words learned. Again, learning appears to account for upward and
downward transfers considerably better than aptitude.

Our findings indicate that learning in all likelihood represents a substantial and justifiable basis for teachers transferring children from group
to group. They also suggest, contrary to the statements of critics, that
grouping does not necessarily represent the assignment of children to
social categories from which they can never extricate themselves. We

are in no position to say that no children are inappropriately assigned or that there are no cases of children languishing in low groups for improper reasons. But there is reason to believe that teachers respond to how well children do in deciding to transfer them upward and downward, and it is not unlikely that those above their group mean in learning who do not transfer may not have made enough progress to justify a move. Moreover, the fact that learning rather than aptitude is more strongly related to transferring suggests that teachers monitor learning progress fairly closely and do not simply fixate on a presumed indication of capacity that led to the assignment of children to groups in the first place.

Changes in Group Characteristics

The most conspicuous difference between fall and spring classes is that in some the number of instructional groups remained the same while in others a group has been added. In no class does the number of groups decline. Classes with one group in the early fall use two groups starting in the late fall or early winter. Those with two groups in the fall use either two or three in the spring, and those with three in the fall employ either three or four in the spring.

In all classes, teachers redistribute children from one group to another after the beginning of the year. Some send them to higher or lower existing groups; others shift members out of existing groups to establish new spring groups. By virtue of these individual transfers and changes in group number, teachers appear to respond to changes in individual learning, to difficulties in the instructional management of certain kinds of groups, or to both.

Traditional grouping change. The nine classes starting the year with traditional ability grouping are distinguishable into two kinds: those with very large numbers of low aptitude children (02, 05, and 10) and those with much smaller numbers (01, 03, 04, 09, 11, and 12), as shown in table 4.8.

As we now know, teachers with large numbers of low aptitude children create large low groups, which almost necessarily entail classes with equal sized groups. Whether teachers create equal sized groups as a matter of preference is moot when the number of low aptitude children is large. The composition of their classes constrains them to accommodate these low aptitude children whether they prefer to or not, and creating a large low group is a reasonable way to do so. By the spring, as table 4.8 shows, classes 02 and 10 have undergone an organizational change: both have added a new low-middle group that draws from both the low and average fall groups. The reason they do so is most likely because smaller groups provide teachers with greater opportunities for more intensive instruction, closer supervision, and greater support of

TABLE 4.8
Group Sizes in Classes in Schools A, B, D, and E, Fall and Spring

School	Class	Class Size	Number Low Aptitude Children	Group Size (Fall)					Group Size (Spring)				
				Low		Avg		High	Low		Avg		High
A	01	37	11	9	—	13	—	15	9	—	4	—	24
B	02	35	19	11	—	13	—	11	5	8	11	—	11
	03	36	8	4	—	14	—	18	4	—	8	10	14
	04	30	10	—	—	5	—	10	—	—	10	—	5
D	05	35	22	13	—	13	—	9	13	—	9	—	13
	09	27	9	2	—	11	—	14	2	—	4	—	21
	10	27	17	10	—	7	—	10	7	7	3	—	10
E	11	28	4	4	—	16	—	8	4	—	8	8	8
	12	29	6	16	—	—	—	13	13	—	10	—	6

the children's work. The teacher in class 05 does not form an additional group; she retains the original three, including the large one of low aptitude. She does, however, change the composition of the middle and high groups by shifting children from the former to the latter, a pattern of change that we will encounter again.

The remaining six classes have small numbers of low aptitude children, and among them, five (01, 03, 04, 09, and 11) have small low groups. For reasons not altogether clear, class 12 has a large low group. Among these five classes (exclusive of class 12), classes 01 and 09 change from fall to spring by moving large numbers of children from the middle to the high group. This pattern suggests that the teachers do not feel terribly burdened by the demands of the low group and as a result can devote energy and time toward moving the higher aptitude children along. Or perhaps this pattern indicates a preferential commitment to the higher aptitude children or alternatively that the teachers' talents are better suited to instructing more able children. We do not know for sure. Note that a similar but less pronounced pattern holds for the teacher in class 05, which has a large low group.

While the teachers of classes 01 and 09 create large high aptitude groups in the spring, those in classes 03 and 11 create new average-high groups (see table 4.8). What distinguishes these four classes is the preoccupation of teachers with the upper end of the aptitude range. They appear to design alternative instructional group arrangements for the more able children when the lower end of the aptitude range does not create massive difficulties in management and instruction. Class 05 may fit this pattern despite its large low group if the teacher is very competent or if she has written the low group off.

These findings show how the nature of grouping established at the beginning of the year influences the pattern of group change later on. Of the three classes that started with large low aptitude groups, two added a new low-average group that reduced the size of the original low group. By contrast, classes that started the year with small low groups underwent changes among the higher aptitude groups. Two classes added new high-average groups, and two others retained the same number of groups but considerably expanded the size of the fall high group. Large initial low groups (or the class properties leading to them such as a large number of low aptitude children) seem to create later teacher preoccupations with the low aptitude end of the class while small initial low groups (or their related class properties) create later preoccupations with the high aptitude end.

Of the nine classes, two remain unaccounted for: 04 and 12. As indicated earlier, class 04 is a special case of a mixed first and second grade class with only the first graders included in our sample. The teacher's grouping pattern in both fall and spring is difficult to make sense of because we have only a partial sample of the class. Class 12 is unusual in that the teacher established only two groups in the fall: high and low. Although it contains few low aptitude children, the teacher nevertheless created a large low group. Why she did not use three groups in the fall (like her colleague in class 11) remains unclear. Establishing a middle group in the spring represents, perhaps, a reversion to what she might have done initially in the fall.

The grouping configurational indices of the nine classes for fall and spring are contained in table 4.5. Comparing the size inequality indices for the two time periods shows that they remain similar in some classes, but change in others. Our prior discussion helps us to understand these varying indices. Classes in which a substantial number of children were moved upward to a high group (classes 01 and 09) show a marked increase in inequality of group size. Those classes in which a new high-average group was formed (classes 03 and 11) display a decrease in size inequality because equalization in size among the higher groups occurred and the three high groups became more similar in size to the smaller low group. Finally, classes forming a new low-average group (classes 02 and 10) were characterized by a slight increase in size inequality because at least one of the newly constituted groups was smaller than the other groups.

Table 4.9 shows correlation coefficients for the relations between fall and spring configurational properties. As anticipated, given the varied patterns of group reformation during the school year, the coefficient for the relation between fall and spring size inequality is relatively low and not significant.

By contrast, substantial relations exist between the fall and spring indices of the other configurational properties, with the number of groups and the range of group means achieving statistical significance. This indicates that the initial properties of the grouping configuration, with the exclusion of relative group size, tend to mark the character of the grouping arrangement for the entire school year. Teachers who form more groups in the fall continue with the same number or form still more during the remainder of the year; and reciprocally, those who begin with few groups continue to have fewer than the other teachers.

Similarly, teachers who begin with highly discrete groups tend to continue with discrete groups, most likely because the composition of the groups remains the same. Further, as the table shows, those teachers who begin the school year with widely differing groups as indicated by the range of group means tend to increase the discreteness of their groups over the remainder of the year. Perhaps children who are inapppropriately assigned to groups, such as low aptitude children assigned to high groups, become more conspicuous when groups and

TABLE 4.9

CORRELATION COEFFICIENTS BETWEEN THE CONFIGURATIONAL PROPERTIES OF
TRADITIONALLY GROUPED CLASSES, FALL AND SPRING (n = 9)

Fall Configurational Properties	Spring Configurational Properties			
	Number of Groups	Size Inequality	Discreteness	Range of Group Means
Number of Groups	0.67*	0.00	0.09	0.10
Size Inequality	−0.20	0.33	−0.37	−0.29
Discreteness	−0.08	0.18	0.47	0.44
Range of Group Means	0.13	0.01	0.82**	0.80**

* $p < 0.05$.   ** $p < 0.01$.

their instruction differ widely, and this leads the teachers to form more homogeneous groups that differ more in mean aptitude.

Finally, the range of group means shows marked stability. This feature of the grouping configuration reflects the diversity of the class, which does not change over the year, and the degree of group discreteness, which is also stable.

Grade-wide grouping change. School F presents a variation of traditional grouping that combines elements of grade-wide grouping into classes and ability grouping within them. Two classes (13 and 14) contain large contingents of able children combined with very small numbers of low aptitude ones. The third class (15) consists of the middle aptitude range of the grade. The teachers in classes 13 and 14 have small numbers of low aptitude children; not surprisingly, they use small groups. They resemble their counterparts in classes 01 and 09, keeping their small low groups intact while transferring middle and high aptitude children. Children transfer both within and between classes. Class 14 retains its three groups, and class 15, which starts with one class-sized group, divides into two, a smaller low-average and a larger average one. Despite the grouping of classes within the grade in school F, the same sorts of forces appear to govern the rearrangement of groups as do in the more traditional arrangement.

Class 15 presents a situation we will also find in school C: the instability of a single, large, diverse instructional group. That class, with thirty-six members and a very large contingent of low aptitude children, divides into two unequal sized, overlapping, low-average and average groups. What is peculiar about this new arrangement is that the low aptitude children remain in the large group with the exception of a batch that moved to classes 13 and 14. Why should this happen? Most likely, we suggest, it is because the new, small group is composed of the whole contingent that was transferred out of the average group in class 14 in addition to a number split off from the original group in class 15. Social as well as learning considerations may have had a bearing on the formation of this group. It is not clear whether this grade-wide pattern is any better than internal class patterns. It appears susceptible to the same pressures generated by large instructional groups, and low aptitude children are dealt with in much the same way.

Delayed grouping change. The only change occurring in school C is from whole class instruction to a two-group pattern, and it is debatable whether to call this a change or rather the initial formation of groups. Once groups are established, however, their properties remain unchanged and there are no transfers of individuals between them. The case does suggest, however, that very large instructional groups are vulnerable to fission even in the face of teacher preferences for instructing all children similarly. Very large groups do not appear to be viable instructional units because of the wide aptitude variations they contain. This is the same pattern we found in class 15.

SUMMARY

The preeminent point about ability grouping is that it pertains to the way classrooms are arranged *for* instruction; it must not, therefore, be confused with direct instructional influences on individual learning. This means that the conventional research that compares homogeneous and heterogeneous classes for their direct impact on learning falls conceptually wide of the mark because it omits the intervening connection between a class outcome, such as a grouping arrangement, and an individual outcome, such as learning. That connection consists of instructional activities for which the groups were formed in the first place. Instruction and grouping are not the same thing. Instruction takes place *in* groups and, among other things, pertains to the way groups are used.

Grouping is also one of a variety of ways by which individual students are allocated to the various levels of school systems. They are assigned to schools by residential location (and sometimes by race); to grades by age; to high school tracks by interest, family background, aspirations, and anticipations of future life chances; and to classes and groups within them by ability. Because groups differ in size, in number, and in their internal distributions of children's characteristics, we find it difficult to conclude that groups are formed primarily in order to adapt instruction to individual differences. There is a stronger case to be made that teachers create groups in response to how abilities and other characteristics are distributed in classrooms. Grouping does, of course, have implications for the individualization of instruction, but those implications are complex.

If groups are made small to increase opportunities for close and concentrated individual attention, they will also be numerous; and the more groups there are, the more time each child must spend doing relatively unsupervised seatwork outside a small group setting. Essentially, grouping involves trade-offs between different kinds of instructional arrangements, and it is difficult to tell whether instruction is more individualized when a teacher spends thirty minutes working closely with eight children and a basal reader or when children are working by themselves at their own pace, with very little supervision, waiting for their group's turn with the teacher. When we think of the real constraints operating in classrooms, the notion of dealing with individual differences loses much of its conceptual bite.

Whatever the group arrangement used, individual differences do get recognized and dealt with, though not in the way a tutorial arrangement of considerable time duration would deal with them. The critical constraint in classroom grouping is that a teacher must make provision for those children not in the group during the time he or she is instructing the group; and the smaller the group under direct instruction, the larger the remainder that needs to be kept productively occupied without direct teacher attention. Grouping, then, is a solution to the problem of finding a workable way to manage a class so that instruction can be carried out; managing individual differences is then one of the by-products of the solution, but that management always takes place in one kind of collective setting or another.

As noted earlier, we found grouping to be a response to the classroom distribution of children's characteristics. The evidence for this gives credence to the formulation of school production that sees events occurring at one level bearing on what happens at other levels—in this case, the influence of class properties on group characteristics. Inherent in the process of arranging a class for instruction is the creation of groups and by definition their properties. Moreover, the linkage between classes and groups is of a conditional nature and not one that lends itself readily to description in linear terms. This is because some kinds of class distributions tightly constrain the available grouping arrangements while others allow teachers leeway to select alternatives consistent with their preferences or proclivities.

Our evidence indicates, finally, that reading groups can be alterable arrangements. We found no support for the idea that groups represent self-fulfilling prophesies, that children expected before the fact to do poorly are left to languish in low groups while those expected to do well are given opportunities to shoot ahead (Rist 1970). The teachers observed in this study moved children from group to group largely on the basis of how well they did. They also changed the grouping arrangements of classes according to the workability of the initial arrangement. That we did not find evidence of vicious classification and discrimination does not mean that it never occurs. The point to be made, however, is that such events are not inherent in the phenomenon of grouping; any social arrangement can be used properly or improperly. We found the teachers in this study to be responding to the distribution of aptitudes in their classes by forming different configurations of groups; and in the next chapter, we will show how they design instruction for the groups that make up these configurations.

5. Group Properties and Content Coverage

At the opening of the school year, teachers are first occupied with the arrangement of the class by establishing different grouping formats. In due course, an initially undifferentiated aggregate of children gets transformed into instructible units, and the instruction of these groupings gets under way. Teachers engage children in learning activities designed at times for everyone together in the class, at other times for small groups under close direction and supervision while the remainder of the class works relatively unsupervised, as well as for individuals working independently. Prevailing classroom conditions—children, instructional materials, time, teacher capacities and goals—are realities that in combination pose problems for teachers and constrain the variety of satisfactory solutions to them that must be worked out on a continuing basis.

Over the course of time, teachers judge the viability of their instructional efforts. They determine not only how well individual children are doing, but also whether the arrangements they have set up work as well as expected. When teachers group children for reading, for example, they solve to some extent the problem of matching the difficulty of materials to the aptitudes of children; but this solution makes teachers less available to direct the work of those children not included in the group being taught, including some who are not able to work on their own. Alternatively, the solution of total class instruction makes teachers equally available to all children and also improves their ability to supervise; but because whole class instruction typically entails the use of a single set of materials, it makes those materials inappropriate for some of the children. In either case, the costs of these grouping arrangements may lead teachers to alter their instruction by changing activities, regrouping children, and redesigning the grouping arrangement of the class, as described in the preceding chapter. We can begin to understand the school year, then, as a series of adjustments that represent more or less appropriate and successful reactions to the progress of instruction itself and to the arrangements designed for carrying it out.

The examples just cited of grouped and whole class instruction pertain to the actual use of class arrangements, and to that extent they go beyond the rather formal analysis of group formation and change presented in chapter 4. Although that analysis faithfully describes and formulates what happened in our fifteen classes, it also represents an abstraction from classroom reality. The social arrangements of a class during instruction are more complex than might be suggested from an analysis simply of the number, relative size, and discreteness of instructional groups.

For reading and language arts activities, usually undertaken in primary classrooms during the morning, several different organizational units, existing both simultaneously and successively, become the focus of instructional planning. The morning, for example, might begin with total class instruction during which seatwork activities undertaken by all class members are explained. Once children begin working on these tasks independently, the teacher assembles the first reading group for work in the basal reader. She might also give a workbook assignment to be completed as seatwork following the small group instruction. Then a second reading group will be called for basal instruction and workbook assignments, and so on through the morning hours until all groups in the class have had their "turn." In that way, some reading activities are planned for the whole class, some for groups within the class, and some for individuals.

To understand reading instruction, we consider two main questions: First, what is the unit and its properties for which instruction is designed (all the members of a class, a group, an individual)? Second, what is the nature of the instruction designed for this unit? Distinguishing between the unit and the instruction planned for it enables us to assess the appropriateness of the match between the aptitudes of children making up the unit and the nature of instructional activities.

There are four components of this matching that must be defined and placed in proper order. Instruction entails (1) a teacher's attempt to adapt

(2) available materials to (3) the characteristics of groups over (4) some period of time. Teachers in effect control and vary the difficulty and amount of materials they assign to groups, the amount of time they allocate, and the extent to which they supervise. Two considerations govern the appropriate matching of materials, time, teacher supervision, and group characteristics. First, is the arrangement appropriate for the group as a whole? Second, is it appropriate for the individuals in each group? With respect to the second consideration, to the extent that a group is diverse in aptitude or other relevant characteristics, an instructional condition (such as a book or worksheet) will be inappropriate for some group members. Instruction appropriate for the group may then be more or less appropriate for the individuals belonging to it, usually depending on the group's homogeneity. As for the first consideration, instruction that is inappropriate for a group is necessarily inappropriate for all its members.

The distinction between the group and individual appropriateness of conditions presumes different criteria for judging the effectiveness of instruction and therefore indicates a need for indices of productivity for both individuals and groups. We have identified an outcome measure that reflects group productivity: content coverage (instructional pace), or how much curricular material is covered over a period of time. Other indices are possible, but we have selected this one because, when treated at the level of individual children, it represents an instructional condition integrally connected with learning.

By using a group index of effectiveness, we address the idea of "appropriateness" in two ways. First, does the outcome match the characteristics of the instructional group? For example, we expect content coverage to accord with the mean aptitude of the group so that groups with abler children will go faster than those with less able ones. Yet, as we will explain later, we do not expect this relation to be simply linear, but rather to be conditioned by the nature of available resources. Second, what are the consequences of a particular match for individual learning? Specifically, to what extent does the amount of material children cover account for how much they learn, and to what degree is the relation between coverage and learning influenced by individual characteristics and instructional conditions? (We treat the latter question in the next chapter.)

Our approach to these questions can be summarized as follows. Instructional design involves the matching of classroom resources (material, time, teaching skill) with the characteristics of instructional groups (the whole class, subgroups within it, or individuals). The appropriateness of the match can be revealed by taking indices of group productivity (content coverage, or pace) and relating them to group characteristics and class resources. In addition, group measures of productivity can be related to other instructional conditions (such as supervision); this set of conditions can then be related to individual outcomes. The remainder of the chapter first develops the formulation conceptually and then deals empirically with the group outcome of content coverage.

CONTENT COVERAGE

We believe that the strongest determinant of what children learn is what they are taught. If they are taught a lot, they will learn a lot. How much material gets presented over a given span of time should influence how much they learn. Nevertheless, the relation between coverage and learning is linear only within limits. As Gates and Russell (1938) demonstrated, the vocabulary burden of first grade materials may be appropriate for children of high readiness, but exceed the capabilities of those of average or low readiness. Indeed, while their high readiness students learned more when they were exposed to a medium or large number of different words, average and low readiness children learned more when they encountered the smallest number of words. That is, they mastered more of a small set of different words and less of larger sets so that their total learning was highest when the vocabulary burden was small.

From the Gates and Russell work, we know in relative terms the size of vocabulary appropriate for children of different readiness. Unfortunately, we do not know exactly how many different words were presented in the course of their study (September to February), and thus cannot identify the point at which the relation between coverage (vocabulary burden) and learning ceased to be linear for different aptitude groups. We do know, however, that perhaps as a response to this work, the vocabulary burden of first grade readers declined from the 1930s to the late 1960s, the time when our study was conducted (see Smith 1965, pp. 279–80).

This work leads directly to the notion of the appropriateness of content covered by children of different ability, and indeed, more recent usage of the term "pace" implies the idea of appropriateness. Carroll, for example, observes that pace can be too fast or too slow: "Some programs present material at such a rapid pace that most students are kept under constant pressure; only the apter students can keep up with this instruction, while the others fall back or out, sometimes never to get caught up. In other programs, the instruction is paced for the benefit of the slower students" (1963, pp. 727–28; see also Harnischfeger and Wiley 1978). Dahlöff (1971) and Lundgren (1972) propose that teachers cover as much content as can be learned by a subgroup of students located in the lower end of the class distribution.

Coverage is important in our research because it represents an outcome of group activities in which the teacher has combined her own talents with the available materials over time. This outcome, moreover, represents a qualitative characterization of the use to which time is put. It is an expression of time that is more than just a metric for recording how long activities last. For example, reading groups meet in classes for about the same amount of time and hence a description of their instructional time does not indicate the real difference in the instruction they experience. By contrast, coverage as a qualitative characterization of that time reveals marked differences among groups in the amount and difficulty of the reading they undertake.

Furthermore, coverage is important because it is a productive condition in its own right, a condition (among others) that influences how much individual children learn (Barr 1983). Because of its pivotal role, its determinants must be identified. While it has been suggested that coverage should be treated as an independent condition (Good, Grouws, and Beckerman 1978), one must not assume that it can be manipulated independently of other conditions, including its own determinants, as a way of elevating the level of learning.

Our position is that instructional groups, formed by teachers in response to the distributive properties of their classes, are the units for which they design instruction; in particular, the different rates at which groups proceed through reading materials are a direct function of the mean aptitude of the respective groups. The match teachers achieve between mean aptitude and assigned materials may also be influenced by three other conditions: the difficulty of the materials, the time allocated by the teacher to different instructional activities, and the teacher's supervision of those activities.

Instructional materials are the source of concepts conveyed and learned. They are a resource that is typically treated as being fixed over the short run of a school year. Thus, if the materials are highly demanding, if they include many new concepts, then it is more likely that children will be exposed to more concepts than if the materials are less difficult.

The time teachers allocate to the use of different materials as well as the activities used to present them also influence content coverage. If a lot of reading time is allocated to phonics skill work and little to basal reading, for example, we expect higher coverage of phonic concepts and lower coverage of basal words. Although such time allocations may reflect total available instructional time, and more specifically that allocated to specific areas such as reading, differential time allocations to specific aspects of reading seem to arise from the preference of teachers.

Finally, how instructional materials are assigned to groups affects instructional pace. The teacher's problem is to bend available materials to provide appropriate instruction to children who vary widely in aptitude. As we have shown in chapter 4, one mode of adapting instruction to the capabilities of children is to create instructional groups. A second is to assign appropriate materials to those groups, usually in a way commensurate with average group aptitude. Assigning too much can overwhelm and lead to low levels of mastery; assigning too little can fail to challenge. Direct supervision of group work facilitates this matching to the extent that teachers have the knowledge necessary to evaluate both group and material characteristics.

The chain of instructional influence, we believe, is from group aptitude to group pace to individual learning. The relation between group aptitude and coverage, moreover, is conditioned by the characteristics of materials, time allocations, and teacher supervision. Similarly, the relation between pace and learning (considered in the following chapter) is influenced by characteristics of the learner, the appropriateness of instruction for the individual, and perhaps supervision as it influences work involvement.

To the extent that pace varies directly with the mean aptitude of instructional groups, it can be judged appropriate in a relative sense. (There is no current basis for determining whether pace is appropriate in an absolute sense.) This means that abler groups proceed more rapidly through materials than less able ones—an obvious but essential indication of instructional appropriateness. Our findings will show, in fact, that there is a strong association between group mean aptitude and coverage. However, while the main proposition is confirmed, the nature of the relation is more complex and interesting than appears on the surface.

EMPIRICAL TEST OF THE FORMULATION

We divide our discussion of the determinants of instructional pace into two parts. In the first, we consider the relation between group characteristics, particularly aptitude, and coverage, and describe the extent to which it holds within classes. In the second, we evaluate the influence of class and instructional conditions on the relation between pace and group mean.

Group Mean Aptitude and Instructional Pace

Instructional pace. Reading materials were described in chapter 3 in terms of the number of new words and phonic concepts they contained. Instructional pace (or coverage) refers to the amount of material actually covered over a given period of time. In our classes, basal pace varied from group to group, and in every case higher ability groups read more basal stories and thus encountered more new words than did less able groups. This was also true for the coverage of workbook materials and the phonics concepts they contained, though with one exception: all students in each class of school B were assigned the same lessons written on the blackboard because workbooks were not provided. Phonics pace is therefore the same for all children in each class. Accordingly, whereas forty-three groups made up our sample for basal instructional planning, only thirty-four groups were considered in the phonics skill work assignments.

Table 5.1 shows the number of new basal words and the number of different phonics concepts covered by groups distinguished by mean aptitude: low, middle, high. When a fourth group was created, we located it between the groups from which the majority of its members originated. A high-middle group, for example, was formed during the year from members of middle and/or high groups. However, in the classes of school C (delayed grouping), we designated the groups as mid_1 and mid_2 although as reported earlier, some difference existed between the average ability of these groups in classes 06 and 07.

School C classes show differences in the number of new words introduced to each group. This difference, which does not exceed fifty words, is trivial compared with the differences separating the low from the high groups in the other two grouping types. The pace of phonics concepts parallels that of word coverage probably because teachers follow the basal manual that recommends that certain pages of phonics skill work be assigned either before or after a story is read.

In the remaining schools (A, B, D, E, and F) we see differences in word coverage by groups in each class that average around two hundred words and in one case (class 03) exceed three hundred fifty words. Clearly, instructional demands differ widely within classes. With one exception, groups ranking higher in ability cover more new words than those ranking lower.

In schools A, C, D, and E differences in phonics coverage parallel those of new word coverage as expected from the differential assignment of phonics exercises to the small groups used for basal reading. In school F, all higher ability groups were expected to cover the same phonics work, while the pace was modified for the lower ability groups. In school B, skill work was assigned to the whole class. The work itself followed the basal teacher's guide recommendation and was appropriate mainly for the high group. Teacher 05, however, who shifted to the Bank Street Readers during the spring of the year, did not introduce additional consonant clusters as would have been expected had her groups proceeded into the first reader of the Scott Foresman series. Thus, phonics pace is lower than expected on the basis of word coverage. Generally, however, we see the influence of the teacher's manual accompanying the basal reading program, which specifies that certain skill pages should be assigned when certain stories are read. In this manner the curricular program embedded in published materials controls the relative introduction of both words and phonics concepts.

Group mean aptitude and pace. The correlation between group mean aptitude and basal word coverage ($r = 0.69$) is higher than that between

TABLE 5.1
Coverage of Basal Words and Phonics Concepts in First Grade Basal Instructional Groups (n = 43) and Phonics Instructional Groups (n = 34)

Grouping Type	School	Class	Coverage of Basal Words						Coverage of Phonics Concepts					
			Low	Low Mid	Mid₁	Mid₂	Mid High	High	Low	Low Mid	Mid₁	Mid₂	Mid High	High
Delayed	C	06	—	—	289	302	—	—	—	—	60	61	—	—
		07	—	—	225	270	—	—	—	—	53	58	—	—
		08	—	—	264	311	—	—	—	—	58	64	—	—
Grade-wide	F	13	69	—	—	—	—	286	44	—	—	—	—	63
		14	18	—	227	—	—	234	44	—	—	—	—	63
		15	—	135	203	—	—	—	44	—	63	—	—	—
Traditional	A	01	100	—	173	—	—	324	12	—	22	—	—	45
	B	02	48	67	170	—	—	255	—	—	44	—	—	—
		03	50	—	124	—	324	422	—	—	45	—	—	—
		04ᵃ	—	—	93	—	—	146	—	—	16	—	—	—
		05	41	—	173	—	—	305	—	—	22	—	—	—
	D	09	160	—	261	—	—	347	40	—	57	—	—	66
		10	249ᵇ	138	180	—	—	347	56	36	42	—	—	66
	E	11	87	—	138	—	195	246	11	—	15	—	28	33
		12	111	—	212	—	—	255	13	—	39	—	—	43

ᵃ Class 04 was composed of less able second graders and more able first graders. We have classified the first grade groups as middle and high because the mean aptitude of the two groups, respectively, was comparable to the middle and high groups in other classes.
ᵇ The teacher shifted from the reading series used by the other children to one with familiar stories in the belief that familiarity would aid learning.

aptitude and phonics concept coverage ($r = 0.43$). Nevertheless, both of these correlations are statistically significant ($p < 0.01$) and lead us to conclude that teachers match instructional pace to the mean aptitude of groups.

At the same time, much variation in instructional pace cannot be accounted for by group mean aptitude since we observe wide differences in new word and phonics concept coverage among groups sharing the same relative rank among classes. For example, the high group in class 02 is introduced to only 255 words while the high group in class 03, in the same school and using the same materials, encounters 422 new words over the year. Among low groups, some are exposed to fewer than 50 words while the pace of others exceeds 100.

When we statistically ruled out the influence of group mean aptitude by calculating residual gain scores, we found some groups paced at rates slower than expected on the basis of aptitude and others paced faster. This indicates, of course, that considerations other than group aptitude determine the coverage of both basal and phonics concepts. Schools C and D, for example, both of which used conceptually denser basal materials, show pacing at a rate higher than expected, presumably because of the more demanding nature of the materials and the greater time spent on them. Conversely, groups in schools E and F, using less difficult basal materials, were paced slower than expected on the basis of mean aptitude. However, a mixed pattern occurs in schools A and B, which also used the less difficult materials: the high and some average groups were paced at a faster than predicted rate, while all the low groups covered less material than expected. While materials and time considerations may account for differences in some classes, they do not account for the mixed patterns found in schools A and B.

We conclude that the mean aptitude of instructional groups is a major determinant of how much material is covered, particularly for basal instruction but also for phonics instruction. At the same time, some of the variance in basal pace (53 percent) is not accounted for by the mean aptitude of basal groups and a substantial proportion of the variance in phonics pace (81 percent) is not accounted for by the mean aptitude of phonics groups. The evidence suggests that materials and time explain some of this variation.

Influence of Instructional Conditions

In chapter 3, we showed that basal materials differed according to the number of new words introduced; the basal materials used by schools C and D presented more new words than those used in the other schools. The same was true with skill work materials. Those used by schools C, D, and F contained more phonics concepts than those used in the other schools.

Estimates of time allocated to basal and skill work activities in different classroom arrangements (total class, small group, seatwork—supervised and unsupervised) were also presented in chapter 3. As an estimation of the total time allocated to basal instruction, we simply summed the time spent in these different settings. For example, as table 3.5 shows, children in class 01 received all their basal instruction in small groups for a total allocated time estimate of twenty-five minutes daily. By contrast, students in class 06 received about fifteen minutes of small group reading, thirty minutes of total class instruction, and twenty minutes of seatwork pertaining to basal activities, for a total allocated time estimate of sixty-five minutes daily. The total time estimates are shown in table 5.2.

Time devoted to the instruction of phonics was more difficult to estimate because phonics work represented only one type of skill activity. To determine what proportion of time devoted to skill activities involved work on phonics concepts, we examined the skill materials used in each class to establish the proportion of total pages that emphasized phonics concepts and studied teacher reports about other materials and tasks used during skill instruction, as shown in table 5.2. We then multiplied the total time allocated to skill work by this proportion to arrive at the total amount of time allocated to phonics activity. For example, in class 01 a total of ninety-five minutes was allocated to skill work as a daily average (see table 5.2) and this multiplied by 30 percent results in an estimated daily time allocation to phonics of twenty-nine minutes. Although instructional groups probably differed in the proportion of time spent on phonics, we have no evidence that permits us to distinguish among them. Therefore, we use the general instructional description provided by teachers to characterize their emphasis on skill work for all groups.

Teacher supervision can influence instructional pace in one of two ways. First, it can result in a more appropriate match between pace and the average aptitude of an instructional group by avoiding the extremes of too rapid and too slow pace. Second, it can result in more allocated time actually being used productively.

The most useful way to characterize teacher supervision is not obvious. For example, it might be described by the *proportion* of total time allocated to a reading activity that is supervised, or by the *absolute* amount of time. Further, it is not clear that the teacher's direction of an instructional activity always provides opportunities for the sort of interaction we envision as producing the proper adjustment between pace and group aptitude. In particular, during small group instruction and supervised seatwork, the teacher examines children's work and provides suggestions; by contrast, during total class instruction, directions are often given for subsequent seatwork, and there is relatively little teacher-pupil interaction connected with ongoing work. We operationalized the concept of teacher supervision by the absolute amount of time during small group instruction and during supervised seatwork. Table 5.2 shows time of supervision in each class based on the time allocations presented in table 3.5.

Yet, it is not only the presence of a teacher that may affect instructional management. Those who spend similar amounts of time in direct supervision may differ considerably in their effectiveness. Because of limitations in our data, which contain little systematic evidence on teacher-pupil interaction during instruction, we cannot directly tell how effective teachers are, for example, in converting allocated time into productive time.

To measure the instructional competence of teachers we included a measure of teaching experience—an index whose remoteness from the concept is considerable—according to the following argument: practical knowledge about teaching is acquired mainly through experience. During each successive year of instruction, teachers learn about different groups of children, about the content of instructional materials, and about teaching methods and classroom arrangements that facilitate class management and children's learning. We expect that a difference between one and two years of experience is of greater significance than that between successive pairs of years because the first year marks the break between no prior experience with full class responsibility and some experience in carrying out an instructional program. Nevertheless, years after the first, up to a point, should contribute some additional knowledge about reading as well as competence in instructional management. Evidence presented in chapter 3 (table 3.6) indicates that each class in our sample has one teacher and that teachers differ considerably in their amount of first grade experience. As we have argued elsewhere (Barr and Dreeben 1978), having experience and making use of it are not necessarily the same thing.

In addition to these conditions, we examine the contribution of two other characteristics of instructional organization. The first is the size of instructional groups; the second is the size of the remainder of the class not in the group. Group size may be taken to represent instructional burdens derived from sheer numbers, on the one hand, and from diversity in aptitude associated with size, on the other. One would expect larger groups to be harder to teach and hence to proceed more slowly.

The size of the class remainder represents the demand from nongroup members on the teacher as she directly instructs a subgroup of the class. Because classes are collective entities, a teacher instructing a group is responsible not only for that group but for planning and managing the activities of the majority not receiving direct attention at the same time. If a class is large and the group receiving direct supervised instruction

TABLE 5.2
Minutes per Day Allocated to Basal, Skill Work, and Phonics Activities and to Teacher Supervision of Basal Reading and Phonics Work

School	Class	Basal Activity	Skill Work Activity	Percent Skill Work in Phonics	Phonics Activity	Teacher Supervision of Basal Reading	Teacher Supervision of Phonics Work
A	01	25	95	30	29	25	3
B	02	20	70	30	21	20	0
	03	50	70	20	14	50	0
	04	25	65	20	13	25	0
	05	25	65	20	13	25	0
C	06	65	85	40	34	25	14
	07	65	85	40	34	25	14
	08	65	85	40	34	25	14
D	09(lo)	30	120	40	48	30	16
	09(mid + hi)	60	90	40	36	30	4
	10	50	100	40	40	50	4
E	11	40	80	20	16	40	0
	12	50	70	20	14	50	0
F	13	50	70	60	42	30	30
	14	45	75	60	45	25	21
	15	50	70	60	42	30	18

is small, the teacher must provide for a very large number of remaining children who in the nature of the case must work without direct supervision. For this reason, the size of the remainder might influence the pace of the instructed group by requiring periodic supervision that detracts from the time available to the smaller group.

For both basal and phonics instruction, we undertook correlational and stepwise regression analyses to determine the contribution of instructional conditions to pace. Conditions were entered into the regression equation according to a statistical criterion: in the order of how much variation in coverage they accounted for. This approach allows us to test the argument that group mean aptitude is the main determinant of coverage and that material difficulty, allocated instructional time, and supervision exert additional influence beyond group aptitude.

Basal instruction and coverage. Table 5.3 shows that five of the seven conditions—group mean aptitude, basal material difficulty, basal instruction time, basal group size, and size of class remainder—are correlated significantly with basal coverage. These correlations, moreover, run in the directions expected. Yet there is one anomalous result in that larger groups proceed at a faster pace than smaller ones. This, however, can be interpreted in light of the association between group size and group aptitude. At least on the basis of the correlational analysis, then, the anomaly appears to be resolved: larger groups go faster because they contain abler children, for reasons explained in chapter 4.

The intercorrelations between these conditions are interesting. First, material difficulty and basal time are highly correlated, indicating that teachers using materials that contain more new words (i.e., are more difficult) allocated more time to basal instruction. In the short run, materials available in the classroom at the beginning of the year appear to influence teachers' allocations of time. In the long run, teacher (or administrator) preferences apparently influence both material selection and time allocation. In any case, the two conditions are collinear in our sample. Accordingly, in subsequent analyses when only one of these conditions accounts for variation in outcomes, it must be remembered that the two—time and materials—work together in their effects.

Table 5.4 shows the results of a stepwise regression analysis in which group mean aptitude, entering in the first step, accounts for 47 percent of the variance in coverage. The difficulty of basal materials, entering in the second step, accounts for an additional 14 percent of variance. Yet, even though harder materials lead to greater word coverage, using them may increase coverage only when accompanied by corresponding time allocations to reading instruction. The correlation of 0.61 (table 5.3) between instructional time and material difficulty illustrates the close connection between these two conditions. It takes more time to deal with harder materials.

TABLE 5.3
CORRELATION MATRIX, MEANS, AND STANDARD DEVIATIONS OF GROUP CHARACTERISTICS, INSTRUCTIONAL CONDITIONS, AND BASAL WORD COVERAGE (N = 43)

	1	2	3	4	5	6	7	8
1 Group Mean Aptitude								
2 Basal Group Size	.43							
3 Basal Material Difficulty	.02	-.20						
4 Basal Instructional Time	.27	.01	.61					
5 Basal Supervision Time	.07	-.22	.04	.34				
6 Grade 1 Teaching Experience	-.10	-.04	-.26	-.01	.35			
7 Size of Class Remainder	-.49	-.64	-.47	-.51	.16	.40		
8 Basal Word Coverage	.68	.37	.39	.42	.11	.05	-.55	
Mean	34.39	10.44	333.67	43.37	33.14	3.79	20.05	199.40
Standard Deviation	15.70	5.93	14.87	14.75	11.13	5.44	7.25	98.11

Levels of significance: 0.05: $r > 0.30$; 0.01: $r > 0.39$.

TABLE 5.4
BETA COEFFICIENTS SHOWING THE CONTRIBUTION OF INSTRUCTIONAL CONDITIONS TO BASAL WORD COVERAGE (n = 43)

Instructional Conditions	Basal Word Coverage						
	I	II	III	IV	V	VI	VII
Basal Group Mean Aptitude	.68**	.67**	.70**	.61**	.62**	.62**	.63**
Basal Material Difficulty		.38*	.44*	.48*	.53*	.54*	.56*
Grade 1 Teaching Experience			.23*	.24*	.26*	.25*	.23
Basal Group Size				.21*	.21*	.22*	.26
Basal Instruction Time					-.07	-.08	-.07
Basal Supervision Time						.03	.03
Size of Class Remainder							.06
R	.68	.78	.81	.83	.83	.83	.83
R² (percent)	47	61	66	69	69	70	70
R² Change (percent)	47	14	5	3	0	1	0
Adjusted R²	45	59	63	66	65	64	64

* Unstandardized coefficient is 2 to 4 times as large as the standard error.

** Unstandardized coefficient is 5 or more times as large as the standard error.

Teaching experience, although uncorrelated with coverage (r = 0.05; table 5.3), when added next, with group aptitude and material difficulty already taken into account, accounts for an additional 5 percent of variance. In the context of those prior influences, more experienced teachers proceed more rapidly than less experienced ones, yet we cannot tell what it is about experience that leads to this result. It may be, for example, that over time teachers realize they can move rapidly where less experience fosters greater timidity. Just as plausibly, experience may lead to better management, which increases usable time and thereby increases pace. Our evidence, however, cannot test our speculations about either the direct or indirect effects of experience.

Finally, basal group size, in combination with the preceding conditions, accounts for an additional 3 percent of variance in coverage. As we suggested in the correlational analysis, the explanation of this relation is not self-evident. Group size, not surprisingly, is substantially correlated with the size of the class remainder (r = −0.64; table 5.3), for if small groups are being instructed, the remainder must be large; how large the remainder will be is determined by the size of the class. But the problem of interpretation here lies in the difficulty of establishing with the available information where the burdens of classroom organization actually reside—in the groups themselves or in the relatively unsupervised and potentially volatile remainder of the class. Thus, the size of groups might not matter very much for establishing pace if the rest of the class is manageable. Large reading groups mean smaller and perhaps more manageable remainders, hence faster coverage of material. Perhaps. However, the two indices of instructional burden are both remote and collinear; therefore, a clear and unequivocal explanation of why group size has a direct influence on coverage eludes us. Note also that while the regression analysis shows group size to affect coverage, the size of the class remainder appears as a weak and statistically insignificant factor. That is undoubtedly because of its substantial correlation with group size as well as with mean aptitude and material difficulty, both of which enter the equation first. This is a case, then, in which collinearity is troublesome; but underlying the problem is both a conceptual and an empirical shortfall in not identifying precisely where the difficulties in grouped instruction lie—to what extent in the properties of the groups themselves and to what extent in the properties of the rest of the class.

Phonics instruction and coverage. Table 5.5 shows that four of the seven conditions—phonics group mean aptitude, phonics material difficulty, phonics instruction time, and supervision time—are significantly correlated with phonics pace. In comparison with basal instruction, group size and the size of the class remainder are only weakly associated with coverage while the supervision of phonics instruction assumes greater importance. These differences make sense when one considers that more phonics instruction occurs as seatwork and that supervised instruction is rare in some classes.

The intercorrelations among material difficulty, instructional time, and supervision are substantial. In fact, because the proportion of phonics exercises used in skill work was used in conjunction with teacher reports to estimate the proportion of skill work time allocated to phonics, our methodology has probably confounded material and time estimates. We did not use the number of different phonics concepts but rather the number of pages pertaining to them. Nevertheless, because those programs covering more phonics concepts also include more work pages to foster their development, there is a high correlation between material difficulty and time allocations estimated in part from the number of workbook pages. In any case, in interpreting the results from the regression analysis, it should be remembered that these three conditions are collinear and therefore work together in producing their effects.

Teachers who set aside a lot of time for phonics also organize instruction so that they are available to supervise the work. However, as observed in the description of basal instruction, time allocations and supervision do not necessarily vary directly. On the basis of mean values reported in tables 5.3 and 5.5, we see that teachers allocate more time to basal reading (forty-three minutes) and supervise a substantial portion of that time (thirty-three minutes). By contrast, less time is spent on phonics activities each day (thirty-one minutes) and considerably less of it is supervised (eight minutes). While there is no reason to argue that more time allocated to an activity necessarily leads to its greater supervision, it is still likely that teachers who value phonics instruction not only set aside more time for it but also believe that their presence facilitates learning. It is also likely that teachers with such preferences secure materials that cover more phonics concepts and provide ample practice exercises.

Table 5.6 shows dramatically the substantial contribution of material difficulty to phonics coverage: it accounts for 59 percent of the variance. Yet, from our previous discussion, we know that material difficulty represents part of an "instructional package" that includes greater time allocated to phonics and an instructional arrangement that permits greater supervision. Accordingly, simply bringing difficult phonics material into a classroom might not increase coverage unless time and supervision are varied appropriately.

Group mean aptitude enters second in the regression equation, and along with material difficulty accounts for an additional 19 percent of the variance in coverage. This means that our formulation, in which coverage is held to respond mainly to the mean aptitude of groups, is not strongly supported, at least not by comparison to basal pace. Indeed,

TABLE 5.5
CORRELATION MATRIX, MEANS, AND STANDARD DEVIATIONS OF GROUP CHARACTERISTICS, INSTRUCTIONAL CONDITIONS, AND PHONICS COVERAGE (n = 34)

	1	2	3	4	5	6	7	8
1 Group Mean Aptitude								
2 Phonics Group Size	.18							
3 Phonics Material Difficulty	.00	-.30						
4 Phonics Instructional Time	-.07	-.29	.87					
5 Phonics Supervision Time	.12	-.10	.66	.74				
6 Grade 1 Teaching Experience	-.03	.41	-.22	-.08	-.09			
7 Size of Class Remainder	-.27	-.81	.04	.29	.11	-.16		
8 Phonics Coverage	.43	.06	.77	.65	.56	-.00	-.25	
Mean	35.97	13.21	56.74	30.62	8.24	2.59	16.15	43.79
Standard Deviation	16.09	9.93	10.03	11.81	8.98	3.66	9.09	17.66

Levels of significance: 0.05: r > 0.35; 0.01: r > 0.45.

TABLE 5.6

BETA COEFFICIENTS SHOWING THE CONTRIBUTION OF INSTRUCTIONAL CONDITIONS TO PHONICS COVERAGE (n = 34)

Instructional Conditions	Phonics Coverage						
	I	II	III	IV	V	VI	VII
Phonics Material Difficulty	.77**	.77**	.84**	.85**	.88**	.84**	.73*
Phonics Group Mean Aptitude		.43**	.39**	.40**	.40**	.41**	.40*
Phonics Group Size			.24*	.20*	.20*	.21*	.11
Grade 1 Teaching Experience				.12	.12	.11	.11
Phonics Supervision Time					-.04	-.07	-.06
Phonics Instruction Time						.07	.16
Size of Class Remainder							-.11
R	.77	.88	.91	.92	.92	.92	.92
R² (percent)	59	78	83	84	84	84	84
R² Change (percent)	59	19	5	1	0	0	0
Adjusted R²	58	76	81	82	81	81	80

* Unstandardized coefficient is 2 to 4 times as large as the standard error.

** Unstandardized coefficient is 5 or more times as large as the standard error.

we were probably in error to think of basal reading, reading skills, and their instruction as separate entities, each of which conforms independently to the formulation. For while basal instruction and coverage follow the formulated argument and accordingly represent essential considerations of instructional design, phonics instruction and coverage are mainly derivative. The latter, in other words, does not appear to be adjusted primarily to the mean aptitude of an instructional group as an independent consideration. Rather, basal instruction is established, and the recommendations of the teacher's manual, in turn, govern phonics coverage. This interpretation is consistent with the dominant influence on phonics coverage imposed by materials. That basal and phonics coverage each have major prior conditions, moreover, is supported by the fact that group mean aptitude and the difficulty of phonics materials have strong and consistent relations with coverage when additional instructional conditions are entered into the regression equations.

Finally, phonics group size, in combination with the preceding conditions, accounts for an additional 5 percent of variance in coverage. As we suggested earlier in our discussion of basal group size, given the substantial correlation between group size and the size of the class remainder, the same problem of interpretation exists here.

SUMMARY

This analysis has shown that once teachers have established reading groups based on children's aptitudes, they turn to the business of providing instruction. In so doing, they use the materials made available to them by the school district. They match these materials to the mean ability level of the groups they have created as indicated by the fact that they have but one set of materials, and for that reason the simplest and most direct way to achieve a match between the difficulty of the materials and the aptitudes of the children is to vary the amount of materials covered. In addition to the matching, the characteristics of the materials themselves—their difficulty—along with time allotments for their use also determine the amount covered over the school year. Harder materials require more time spent on them, and the larger time investment over the course of the year eventuates in greater coverage at the end.

The evidence supports our formulation of instruction as it pertains to basal reading. The major determinant of basal coverage is the mean aptitude of instructional groups. Other conditions exert an influence on it over and above group aptitude, the most substantial of these being the difficulty of basal materials. By contrast, the formulation is only partially supported as it pertains to phonics. The major determinant of phonics coverage is *not* the mean aptitude of the instructional group, but rather the difficulty of phonics materials. But, as discussed earlier, the pattern of relations suggests that it is probably inappropriate to think of reading skills and their instruction as separable entities, each of which conforms to our formulation. Rather, in order to account for the coverage of phonics content, the connection between basal and phonics activities as coordinated by a single reading program must be taken into consideration.

Despite all of this, 32 percent of the existing variance in basal coverage and 20 percent of the variance in phonics coverage are not accounted for by group mean aptitude and other conditions in this formulation. The class-by-class analysis of the pace of instructional groups displays large differences among groups of similar aptitude, particularly among high groups. Thus, while acknowledging the general utility of our formulation, we stress that other considerations, systematic and otherwise, are at work in the determination of pace.

An unanticipated finding relates to the collinearity of instructional conditions. Material difficulty and allocated time were highly correlated in basal instruction; difficulty, time, and supervision were highly correlated in phonics instruction. It seems reasonable that such collinearity should exist; and since it does, assumptions about the independence of instructional conditions must clearly give way to assumptions about conditionality and collinearity.

As we indicated in chapter 4, grouping is often justified as a means of individualizing instruction; but we would argue that it is not very useful to think about the direct relevance of grouping for dealing with differences among individuals. While chapter 4 showed how grouping is a response to the diversity of class composition, this chapter has shown that instruction both is strongly influenced by the characteristics of groups and is independent of them. Thus, even though group mean aptitude is related to the coverage of material, groups of similar aptitude also vary in their coverage, partly in response to the nature of materials and to the allotment of time. Groups, then, are treated differently by teachers in the course of instruction—even similar groups. The independence of instruction from grouping is as important as the connection between them. In addition, instruction is oriented toward groups, not toward individuals. For this reason attempts to find direct connections between grouping and individual differences are conceptually and empirically inappropriate.

Naturally, as a result of their instructional experience in groups, individual children engage in learning activities to varying degrees and approach their schoolwork with different capacities. These are the individual differences, along with grouped instruction, that will determine how much they learn; and it is to this set of questions that we turn in the next chapter.

6. Individual Learning

We turn finally to the matter of how school production results in values created in individuals—specifically, how instruction influences learning. For just as group formation is a productive outcome of class activities and content coverage an outcome of group activities, learning is the most important individual outcome. It is the raison d'être for the whole productive apparatus of school systems, which are there so that children might learn.

In the previous chapters, we were much preoccupied with formulating the nature of school production because in our estimation that task had not previously been undertaken in a systematic and persuasive way, or it had been mistaken for the explanation of individual achievement. Learning and achievement, however, are only part of the story. This chapter deals with learning to read as one kind of achievement and treats two major influences on that outcome: first, the elements of instruction, and second, the characteristics of children.

Our formulation specifies that certain elements of instruction will influence learning; among them, and most importantly, the amount of material covered. But even if coverage turns out to have a strong influence on learning—as indeed it will—we still need to know whether other instructional conditions (discussed in chapter 5) affect learning *directly*

126

over and above their influence on coverage. For example, time allotments may be mediated through content coverage and not affect learning directly, but supervision may turn out to influence both the amount of material that groups cover and individual learning by increasing work involvement.

In addition to instructional conditions, common sense would indicate that characteristics of children themselves influence how much they learn. The most obvious of these characteristics is aptitude, or reading readiness. And while we have already made the case for the importance of aptitude in previous chapters, the case for other characteristics such as age, sex, and socioeconomic status remains to be made. There is a long tradition of reading research in which each of these characteristics is important. Particularly in the early grades, boys on the average learn to read more slowly than girls. In the first grade, children who are young for their grade tend to have greater difficulty starting to read than those who are more mature. Unlike sex and age, socioeconomic status is a less precise concept that serves as a proxy for a variety of influences originating in the home and the community. It provides a loose summary of conditions such as wealth and family resources, parental support and interest, artifacts in the home, parental and community pressure that together are a global indication of a more or less favorable environment for learning.

In chapter 3, we showed how instructional conditions varied at different locations in the school system but without any clear sense of how they were tied together to influence learning. In this chapter, we shall try to identify the sequence of influence among those conditions, paying special attention to the distinction between instruction, which is an element of organizational functioning, and children's characteristics, which represent their own contributions to their own learning. To confound these two sources of influence is fatal.

If an outcome such as learning is expressed at the individual level, then the immediately associated conditions that produce it must be treated at the same level. Conditions of learning, then, refer to the experiences of children in their encounters with books and other materials, their location in groups and classes, their dealings with teachers and engagement in classroom activities, and their background characteristics ·and capacities for learning. For example, while all children "have" aptitudes as individual characteristics, they do not have an instructional pace in the same sense because pace is a group property. Nevertheless, all children belonging to an instructional group proceed at a given pace and for that reason have the experience of going through material at the group pace by virtue of their membership. In this way, pace as well as other group and class properties can be expressed as individual experiences and thus can be related to learning even though pace itself is a group property.

We are concerned with two different kinds of learning outcomes: immediate learning specific to the content of the material taught; and general reading achievement, which is relatively more independent of specific curricular content. Further, we use two measures of content-specific learning, one pertaining to basal words, the other to phonics.

Basal word tests were designed for instructional groups. Information obtained from teachers in May indicated where each group was reading in the basal reader and thus the number of different words to which it had been exposed. To determine how well children had learned the words, a random word sample was selected that included some words each child had not yet encountered (to establish a ceiling on learning). The number of words correctly identified on the test was used to estimate the total words learned.

Phonics learning was assessed by an informal test involving the pronunciation of syllables. The same test, administered to all children, contained fifteen items with an equal number of two-, three-, and four-letter syllables, and it was scored on the basis of correctly pronounced phonemes and observation of vowel markers. Both measures of content-specific learning were administered to children individually in order to increase validity.

Two aspects of general reading achievement were measured by the Gates-MacGinitie Reading Tests (1965). The vocabulary section of the test demands recognition of printed words occurring as isolated units that correspond to a picture. The comprehension section involves reading short passages and selecting a picture that conveys their meaning. The Primary A test was administered at the end of first grade, and Primary B at the end of second grade.

The content-specific measures of learning are useful because of their sensitivity to the effects of instructional conditions, while the combination of the two types of outcome measures allows us to examine the contribution of specific content learning to the development of more general skills. Indeed, the evidence presented on specific content learning would be of only limited interest if it could not be demonstrated that it influences general reading achievement. In fact, basal word learning is highly correlated with reading achievement measured by the standardized test at the end of first grade ($r = 0.83$) and second grade ($r = 0.75$). Similarly, the correlation coefficients between phonics learning and first and second grade reading achievement, respectively, are substantial ($r = 0.76$ and 0.70). These strong positive relations are exceedingly important (even though they are expected) because they indicate that our curriculum-specific measures of learning are sensitive to reading skills that are components of general and nationally recognized criteria of reading achievement.

Once the instruction of a particular skill or content domain is in progress, children's achievement must be assessed for a particular grade level in terms of what has been learned during that year. Typical methods for accounting for the proficiency of children when they begin a school year include the use of residual or simple gain scores or covariation of initial scores. By contrast, in first grade reading instruction, initial capabilities need not be accounted for if most children begin learning to read in the first grade, as was the case for our sample. Their measured skill on reading tests was both similar and negligible. One can nevertheless view reading acquisition in a broader perspective that includes language acquisition, picture and symbol recognition, phoneme and syllable recognition, and phoneme and syllable discrimination. Given this view, it would be appropriate to treat readiness measures as indices of the capabilities with which children begin first grade.

We decided to view reading acquisition more narrowly as referring to the development of skill in comprehending English orthographic symbols. Tests administered at the end of kindergarten or the beginning of first grade revealed that none of the children in our study sample could read, although a small number of children in the classes but not in our sample possessed limited proficiency. Thus, it is fair to assume that reading skill assessed at the end of first grade reflects the interaction of children's ability to learn and the instructional conditions prevailing during the school year. Although the children all shared a very low level of reading proficiency—that is, they could not read—they nevertheless differed considerably in their aptitude for learning to read, as indicated by our readiness measure. Therefore, had we covaried aptitude, we could not have determined how these differences in readiness, along with instruction, contributed to learning.

In our analysis of learning, we address three main questions. First, to what extent does the amount of content covered influence learning? In chapter 5, we argued that the importance of coverage as a central component of school production could be demonstrated in part by its influence on individual learning. The strong influence of coverage on learning is not, however, a new finding. It was reported by Barr (1973–74) in a study of three of the six schools (B, C, and D) in the present sample. And while that earlier work demonstrated a dramatic group effect, it was not set in a broader context of school production in which class, group, and individual phenomena were tied together in a single formulation.

Second, what instructional conditions besides the coverage of content impinge directly on learning? As previously indicated, this analysis pertains to conditions derived from our analysis of school production.

Third, how do the characteristics of individual children and the nature of instructional conditions come together to affect learning? Consider the case of aptitude. As an individual characteristic, aptitude is expected to have a direct connection with learning; this is because performance in an activity should be strongly influenced by the capacities relevant to that activity. But aptitude also figures into the picture of school production in another way because teachers take the aptitude distribution of classes into account in forming groups, whose mean level of aptitude determines instructional pace. We will attempt, then, to disentangle the effects of aptitude as an individual characteristic pure and simple from aptitude as an organizational element shaping the conditions of instruction. Further, we consider other instructional conditions besides aptitude through the various manifestations of children's experience that affect their learning.

INFLUENCE OF CONTENT COVERAGE ON LEARNING

In our formulation of school production, content coverage is the major outcome of instructional groups; by virtue of that, it is also a key instructional condition shaping the experience of individual children. Indeed, our evidence shows that pace is a major influence upon learning: the more material children cover, the more they learn. As shown in table 6.1, the correlation coefficient of 0.93 indicates that basal coverage accounts for 86 percent of the variance in basal word learning. Further, basal coverage is a strong predictor of reading achievement measured at the end of first grade ($r = 0.75$) as well as at the end of second grade ($r = 0.71$), where the measure of achievement consists of a raw vocabulary score and a raw comprehension score which are standardized and combined. Phonics coverage accounts for a substantial proportion of the variance in phonics learning (38 percent) and is significantly correlated with reading achievement at the end of both the first ($r = 0.57$) and second grades ($r = 0.52$). Thus, under the conditions prevailing in our fifteen classes, the more material children covered, the more they learned, although that generalization holds more strongly for basal than for phonics learning. Further, content coverage, and its associated learning during first grade, continues to influence reading performance during the second year of instruction as indicated by the high correlation between first and second grade reading performance. This latter is an exceedingly important result because it testifies to the stability of the relation as it is reinforced by second grade instruction.

Table 6.2 presents descriptive evidence concerning the average learning and mastery of basal words along with the phonics learning of instructional groups, showing how well the groups perform. Average basal word learning varies widely from group to group, consistently with variation in basal coverage. In school C, where groups were paced

TABLE 6.1
CORRELATION MATRIX OF COVERAGE AND LEARNING (n = 147)

	1	2	3	4	5	6
1 Basal Coverage						
2 Phonics Coverage	0.51					
3 Basal Learning	0.93	0.50				
4 Phonics Learning	0.51	0.62	0.60			
5 First Grade Achievement	0.75	0.57	0.83	0.76		
6 Second Grade Achievement	0.71	0.52	0.75	0.70	0.89	
Mean	228.7	46.3	190.0	19.7	0.0	0.0
Standard Deviation	100.0	15.8	105.6	13.5	1.9	1.9

Levels of significance: 0.05: $r > 0.17$; 0.01: $r > 0.23$.

most similarly, we observe less difference in learning than in the other schools.

Beneath the word learning averages are shown mastery percentages derived by dividing the average group learning by the basal coverage of the group. For example, the low group in class 01 learned 68 words on the average from the 100 words presented during first grade, yielding an average percent mastery of 68. Although the degree of correlation between content coverage and learning is extremely high ($r = 0.93$), the mastery percentages show that many groups do not master all that has been presented. Lower aptitude groups, as expected, master less than those containing abler children. The mastery percentages are lower in school B groups than in other schools, with some high as well as low groups showing relatively low levels of mastery. It is interesting to note that the groups in the split grade 1–2 class (class 04) covered relatively little in their basals and mastered less than half of it.

Table 6.2 also shows the average phonics scores of the same groups. Schools C, D, and F, which used more difficult phonics materials, are characterized by higher phonics learning. Generally, differences among groups reflect the phonics content covered by them with the exception that able readers learn phonics concepts at a relatively high level even when relatively few concepts are introduced.

There is strong evidence from these results that as basal and phonics coverage varies in classes by groups, so does basal and phonics learning. Basal mastery also varies by group, but not so dramatically as basal words learned and phonics concepts acquired.

INFLUENCE OF OTHER INSTRUCTIONAL CONDITIONS ON LEARNING

Although we have just shown the strong connection between the coverage of materials (as related to group placement) and learning, there

TABLE 6.2
NUMBER OF BASAL WORDS LEARNED AND PERCENTAGE MASTERED IN BASAL GROUPS (n = 43) AND PHONICS CONCEPTS LEARNED IN PHONICS GROUPS (n = 34)

Grouping Type	School	Class	Basal Groups						Phonics Groups					
			Low	Low Mid	Mid₁	Mid₂	Mid High	High	Low	Low Mid	Mid₁	Mid₂	Mid High	High
Delayed	C	06	—	—	259 90%	272 90%	—	—	—	—	30	18	—	—
		07	—	—	157 70%	245 91%	—	—	—	—	20	31	—	—
		08	—	—	235 89%	300 96%	—	—	—	—	26	35	—	—
Grade-wide	F	13	64 93%	—	—	—	—	274 96%	15	—	—	—	—	38
		14	5 28%	—	166 73%	—	—	214 91%	9	—	30	—	—	35
		15	—	83 61%	155 76%	—	—	—	—	22	30	—	—	—
Traditional	A	01	68 68%	—	154 89%	—	—	314 97%	0	—	2	—	—	25
	B	02	17 35%	27 40%	138 81%	—	—	217 85%	0	3	9	—	—	24
		03	26 52%	—	76 61%	—	246 76%	370 88%	0	—	8	—	1	24
		04	—	—	41 44%	—	—	65 45%	—	—	7	—	—	6
		05	27 66%	—	99 57%	—	—	188 62%	5	—	4	—	—	7

TABLE 6.2 (continued)

Grouping Type	School	Class	Basal Groups						Phonics Groups					
			Low	Low Mid	Mid$_1$	Mid$_2$	Mid High	High	Low	Low Mid	Mid$_1$	Mid$_2$	Mid High	High
D		09	85 53%	—	199 76%	—	—	298 86%	18	—	17	—	—	27
		10	85 34%	104 75%	180 100%	—	—	347 100%	15	5	17	—	—	38
E		11	70 80%	—	107 78%	—	179 92%	209 85%	4	—	17	—	17	28
		12	85 77%	—	198 93%	—	—	250 98%	14	—	24	—	—	38

Note: Mastery refers to the words children learn as a percentage of those they cover.

is reason to believe that other instructional conditions influence learning as well. For example, as shown in appendix F, material difficulty and instructional time are correlated with learning. An interesting question is whether these other conditions exert their impact through coverage, which in turn influences learning, or whether they influence learning directly. Consider the case of the difficulty of materials. An earlier discussion in chapter 5 reveals that the more difficult the materials, the more concepts introduced over the school year; and this in all likelihood is because teachers spend more time on them. Accordingly, we would argue that the nature of the instructional materials influences learning through the amount of materials actually covered.

Other conditions, however, such as supervision and class size might influence learning directly over and above any influence on coverage. It therefore becomes important to disentangle these instructional influences by investigating other conditions in addition to coverage that might influence learning. To do this, we undertook a stepwise regression analysis in which coverage was entered into the equation first. Additional conditions were then entered according to a statistical criterion—not a substantive one, as was the case with coverage—namely: in the order of how much variation in learning they accounted for. This approach is consistent with our formulation, which assigns primary conceptual importance to coverage but which is unable to determine an ordering of the other conditions.

Suppose, however, that we did not enter coverage into the equation first (thus almost guaranteeing its predominant influence on learning) but instead entered it on the same basis as the other conditions to seek its own level according to its contribution to learning. We discovered that there was no difference in the case of basal learning because coverage is the condition most highly correlated with learning. Similarly, there was no difference in the case of phonics learning for the total sample and for the subsample composed of high aptitude students. Thus, we felt justified in entering coverage into the equation first, particularly for basal instruction.

Table 6.3 shows that basal coverage has a massive impact on learning not only for the total sample but for sectors of it distinguished on the basis of individual aptitude. None of the other instructional conditions, which are listed for the total sample in the order they were entered into the stepwise analysis, makes more than a trivial contribution to learning once the effects of coverage have been taken into account. We conclude that other conditions that are significantly correlated with learning exert their influence indirectly through content coverage. This general result holds for subsamples as well as for the total sample.

No such massive impact of coverage on learning is found, however, in the case of phonics, as table 6.4 shows; in the total sample, phonics

TABLE 6.3

PERCENTAGE CHANGE IN VARIANCE IN LEARNING ACCOUNTED FOR BY CONTENT COVERAGE AND OTHER INSTRUCTIONAL, CLASS, AND GROUP CONDITIONS FOR BASAL INSTRUCTION

Instructional, Class, and Group Conditions[a]	Total Sample (n = 147)	Subgroups Based on Aptitude		
		Low (n = 45)	Average (n = 58)	High (n = 44)
Basal Coverage	86	77 (1)[a]	84 (1)	80 (1)
Number Low Aptitude Children	0	0 (3)	1 (2)	1 (4)
Instructional Group Size	0	—[b]	1 (4)	0 (5)
Basal Instruction Time	0	0 (7)	1 (3)	1 (7)
Total Reading Time	0	—	0 (10)	2 (2)
Basal Material Difficulty	0	1 (6)	1 (8)	1 (3)
Length of School Day	0	0 (5)	1 (7)	—
Grade 1 Teaching Experience	0	1 (2)	1 (5)	0 (8)
Class Size	0	1 (4)	0 (9)	0 (6)
Basal Supervision Time	0	—	1 (6)	0 (9)

[a] Conditions are listed for the whole sample in the order they entered into the stepwise regression analysis. The numbers in parentheses show the ordering of variables in each subsample.

[b] When no percentage is shown, the tolerance is too low for the variable to enter the regression equation.

TABLE 6.4

PERCENTAGE CHANGE IN VARIANCE IN LEARNING ACCOUNTED FOR BY CONTENT COVERAGE AND OTHER INSTRUCTIONAL, CLASS, AND GROUP CONDITIONS FOR PHONICS INSTRUCTION

Instructional, Class, and Group Conditions[a]	Total Sample (n = 147)	Subgroups Based on Aptitude		
		Low (n = 45)	Average (n = 58)	High (n = 44)
Phonics Coverage	38	36 (1)[a]	35 (1)	27 (1)
Length of School Day	8	26 (2)	8 (2)	3 (2)
Phonics Material Difficulty	5	5 (3)	1 (4)	8 (3)
Phonics Instruction Time	2	2 (8)	2 (3)	0 (8)
Grade 1 Teaching Experience	1	5 (4)	0 (9)	0 (10)
Number Low Aptitude Children	1	0 (9)	—[b]	1 (4)
Phonics Supervision Time	0	1 (5)	0 (7)	1 (5)
Total Reading Time	2	1 (6)	0 (8)	1 (7)
Phonics Group Size	0	1 (7)	1 (6)	0 (9)
Class Size	0	0 (10)	2 (5)	3 (6)

[a] Conditions are listed for the whole sample in the order they entered into the stepwise regression analysis. The numbers in parentheses show the ordering of variables in each subsample.

[b] When no percentage is shown, the tolerance is too low for the variable to enter the regression equation.

coverage has the largest effect, but not a large one. In addition, the length of the school day and the difficulty of materials are shown to influence learning directly as well as indirectly through coverage. This pattern is found in the high aptitude subgroup; it is also found in the low and average subgroups but only when coverage is entered into the equation first.

In the low subsample, when all instructional conditions, including coverage, were allowed to enter the equation according to the magnitude of their contribution to learning, the order of conditions and the change in learning variance accounted for were as follows: length of school day (55 percent), phonics coverage (7 percent), phonics material difficulty (5 percent), grade 1 teaching experience (5 percent), phonics supervision time (1 percent), total reading time (1 percent), phonics group size (1 percent), phonics instruction time (2 percent), number of low aptitude children (0 percent), and class size (0 percent).

For the average subsample, three conditions were similarly correlated with learning: phonics coverage (r = 0.59), phonics instruction time (r = 0.60), and phonics material difficulty (r = 0.59), as well as being highly intercorrelated. When all instructional conditions, including coverage, were allowed to enter the equation on the basis of the magnitude of their contribution to learning, the order of conditions and the change in learning variance accounted for were as follows: phonics instruction time (37 percent), phonics coverage (6 percent), grade 1 teaching experience (2 percent), length of school day (1 percent), phonics material difficulty (2 percent), class size (1 percent), phonics group size (1 percent), total reading time (0 percent), and phonics supervision time (0 percent).

Thus, the length of the school day is the condition most highly correlated with learning in the low aptitude subsample, while three instructional conditions—phonics instruction time, material difficulty, and coverage—are similar in their correlations with learning for the average subsample, accounting for about 35 percent of the variance. Coverage, then, is *not* the most substantial influence on learning in these subsamples. Nevertheless, when coverage is entered into the equation first, the results for the total sample and the subsamples are similar in showing that daily time and material difficulty contribute notably (table 6.4) in accounting for phonics learning.

That the length of the school day should appear to be strongly associated with phonics learning is rather peculiar. There are, after all, many different things that can happen during a lengthened school day; why should phonics learning then appear as a correlate of such a remote proxy for unspecified influences that length of school day represents? Evidence presented in appendix F sheds some light on this question. The length of the day turns out to be highly correlated with total reading time (r = 0.66) as well as with both time spent on basal instruction (r = 0.74) and time spent on phonics instruction (r = 0.65). These findings tell us that the length of the school day probably does not exert a direct influence upon phonics learning, but rather is a global indicator of a general commitment to reading instruction. In effect, when teachers have a longer day, they spend more time on all sorts of reading activities. This is not necessarily a larger proportion of the day; perhaps it is only the additional time taken up by a constant proportion of a larger overall time allotment.

Like the length of the school day, time devoted to basal and to phonics instruction is also a rather remote index of instructional activities, for while it signifies the importance attributed to reading, it does not indicate how the time is used to influence learning. The length of the day, however, is associated with instructional activities and in an interesting way. It is correlated significantly (r = 0.60) with the direct supervision of phonics instruction but not with the supervision of basal instruction (r = 0.09). Similarly, the length of the day is related significantly to the coverage of phonics materials (r = 0.48) but not to the coverage of basal materials (r = 0.09).

The fact that the length of the day is related to the supervision of phonics instruction provides a clue to what is happening as well as to the meaning of the variable "length of school day." Work on phonics occurs in two ways: as seatwork in which it is largely unsupervised, and as a group activity in which it is closely supervised, just like grouped basal instruction. As we already know, basal reading instruction is the core of the reading program in these schools; phonics is added on and derivative. But with a longer school day, teachers appear to extend the time used for supervised phonics instruction. The length of the day, then, seems to measure by proxy the time available beyond that employed in supervised basal instruction. When that additional time afforded by an extended school day is available, some teachers appear to use it for supervised phonics instruction in groups.

Why teachers might value such additional phonics time can be seen when we compare the amount of time available for both kinds of reading instruction and the amount of time devoted to supervision. On the average, teachers allocated forty-four minutes each day to basal instruction but only twenty-eight minutes to phonics. And while basal instruction is supervised for an average of thirty-two minutes per day, phonics is supervised for only eight. Additional time available for supervised phonics instruction, under these circumstances, is valued. While the amount of phonics supervision might not matter too much once a minimum threshold has been reached, there may still be a low critical point below which unsupervised work actually interferes with learning, especially among children who need the supervision most. By contrast, supervision and time allocated to basal reading might be sufficiently above the minimum in our sample that variation in them is unrelated to learning.

Particularly among the low aptitude children, the longer the day, the more they learn. Not only does daily time in combination with coverage account for 26 percent more variance in learning than coverage by itself, but when it is entered into the equation first it alone accounts for 55 percent of the variance. Therefore, the lengthened school day and the sort of phonics program it permits appear to have special value for low aptitude children.

We expected material difficulty to influence learning only indirectly through coverage; indeed, this was true for basal instruction and learning. We do not know how material difficulty acts as a direct influence on phonics learning, although a possible explanation may be that materials that contain more new phonics concepts also include more activities and practice that reinforce learning. Accordingly, children who cover fewer concepts in materials that include not only more concepts but also more explanation and practice may learn more of the concepts introduced than those children covering more with less supportive materials. This interpretation suggests that it may be useful to characterize instructional materials along other dimensions besides the number of concepts introduced.

Although daily time and the difficulty of phonics material, along with coverage, account for a substantial percentage of learning variance generally, a final condition—the experience of the teacher in grade 1—contributes significantly to learning variation among low aptitude children. The negative correlation coefficient between teacher experience and phonics learning ($r = -0.26$) indicates that less experienced teachers realize more success in phonics learning than do the more experienced. We are not certain why this relation appears, but it may be that inexperienced teachers value phonics instruction and have not "written off" the low aptitude children as unteachable. We must also acknowledge that our data do not permit us to explore the meaning of our variable "teaching experience."

In sum, in the light of our prior analysis of school production, we find that the group outcome of instructional pace, when specified to the individual level as a condition of learning, has a massive impact on children's learning of the curricular material presented to them. This generalization holds solidly with respect to the content of basal readers; it holds to a less substantial extent with phonics learning. In addition, instructional pace far overwhelms other instructional influences on basal learning, for the sample as a whole and for subsamples based upon aptitude. Instructional conditions other than coverage make more of a difference in phonics than in basal learning.

Disentangling the Effects of Instruction and Children's Characteristics

The collinear relation we discovered between aptitude and coverage in chapter 3 indicates a need to explore in greater detail the influences on learning that emanate from individual children themselves and those that derive from instruction. The distinction is important because it separates those components of the learning situation that derive from individual characteristics and are fixed in the short run from those that are variable and fall under the control of teachers.

Our problem is to identify characteristics of individuals and of instruction that represent basic conditions of learning. Although aptitude is an obvious influence, it can readily be confounded with certain background characteristics that knowledge of the status attainment process shows to be associated with learning. Most important among these are socioeconomic status, which is an indication of parental support, of household resources, and of interest in children's schooling; and age and sex, both of which are known to be important considerations in early reading.

What conditions should be selected to represent classroom instruction? In accord with our analyses in the two preceding chapters, we select two properties of instructional groups, their size and mean aptitude, as well as content coverage to represent primary instructional influences. Chapter 4 revealed the substantial collinearity among content coverage, material difficulty, and time allocation. Accordingly, coverage is interpreted as an instructional outcome that reflects the materials teachers have to work with and their allocation and management of instructional time.

We have already seen how instructional components are shaped as teachers establish groups in classes and then proceed through learning materials in the groups they have created. But now that the discussion turns to individual learning and to the characteristics of individuals conducive to learning, we need to express instructional influences, not as class and group properties, but as elements of individual experience. Accordingly, group size in this analysis refers not to the size of groups but rather to children's experiences in groups of different sizes. Similarly, coverage refers not to the pace at which the teachers take the children through their basal readers and phonics materials, but to children's experience in covering material quickly or slowly by virtue of their membership in groups.

There are times when the association between conditions of learning seems to be both conceptually and empirically appropriate. Such is the case between the difficulty of materials and the time devoted to learning them. The harder the materials, the more time spent. We do not think of this kind of collinearity (in the explanation of coverage) as a source of error, but rather as reflecting a reality in which explanatory conditions actually occur together. Conceptually, the relation we found earlier between aptitude and coverage, an individual capacity and an instructional condition, strikes us as of a different order because the origins of the two influences are so different. For that reason we will attempt to determine whether they are actually correlated or whether they contribute to learning in different ways.

In the preceding section of this chapter, we showed how the coverage of material appears as the strongest determinant of learning. This is true markedly in basal instruction but less so in phonics. The latter, as we indicated earlier, has a derivative connection to the former; and so its weaker connection to learning is understandable. In identifying the distinct contributions of individual characteristics and instructional conditions, aptitude and coverage must enter the picture. And because background characteristics other than aptitude, such as socioeconomic status, age, and sex, have been found to affect learning, we must include them not only to gain an uncontaminated measure of aptitude, but to determine whether they affect learning over and above aptitude and the elements of instruction.

We have included the size of basal groups because our evidence from chapter 4 indicates that teachers vary the size of groups over the course of the year to accommodate those children who are progressing well, who are often moved into large high aptitude groups, and those who are experiencing difficulty, who are kept in small groups. The variation in group size, then, appears to be an important element of instructional organization, but with different meaning for the more and less able children. Finally, we expect the mean aptitude of groups to influence coverage, which in turn will influence the learning of words and of phonics concepts; they will then influence first grade achievement.

We have employed path analytic techniques both to express this sequence of instructional developments and to trace the respective influences of aptitude and instruction on learning. Conceptually, this is an analysis of status attainment (see chapter 2) where the attainment in question is the near term outcome of reading achievement. The question is whether this outcome is the product of individual capacities, the ascriptive characteristics of social background, or those productive elements of school organization that constitute instruction.

We present our findings in a correlation matrix (table 6.5) upon which both regression analyses (table 6.6) and a path analysis (figure 6.1) are based. All are calculated for the complete sample of 147 children. The regression table presents all (standardized) beta coefficients, and the path diagram shows only those paths whose unstandardized regression coefficients are two or more times the standard error. We do not claim, however, that small coefficients necessarily have little importance because they are small. Indeed, the path analysis shows some small coefficients that have great substantive importance, where a relation expected plausibly to be large nevertheless turns out to be small.

A path analysis purports to demonstrate causal linkages between a set of conditions and its consequences. It does this by first defining certain prior conditions (exogenous variables) that are taken as given, that is to say, determined by other causes external to the analysis under consideration. They are children's background characteristics and aptitude. Approximations to causality are established by arranging the endogenous variables (a set of dependent variables) in a time sequence so that earlier events are allowed to explain later ones. This time sequence, established empirically and conceptually, determines the order in which variables are entered into regression equations.

Once the exogenous variables and their intercorrelations are included, the endogenous variables are entered in the following order: group size, group mean aptitude, basal coverage, phonics coverage, basal learning, phonics learning, and first grade achievement. While there is a clear, empirically demonstrable temporal ordering that links individual aptitude, group mean aptitude, coverage, and learning for both basal and phonics instruction, the ordering is not quite so clear with respect to group size and group mean aptitude because both of these group properties are established at the same time—when groups are formed. Yet a defensible case can be made for the instructional priority of size. Size is determined the moment the group is formed (and, literally, so is the mean aptitude). But the instructional importance of group mean aptitude does not emerge until later when reading gets under way and teachers begin to adapt the pace of instruction to the aptitude composition of the group.

Although there is no clear temporal ordering between basal and phonics coverage, there is nevertheless a causal ordering (as discussed in chapter 5) because the basal program determines phonics instruction. By contrast, there is no clear causal ordering between basal and phonics learning, and we have simply employed the same order that applies to coverage. The curricular outcomes are simultaneous, but both of them clearly come prior to general first grade achievement. In sum, while every step of the sequence cannot be justified meticulously by time priority, the development of the central argument—the sequence from individual characteristics to group properties to coverage to learning— certainly can.

Turning to the path analysis, note first the very small intercorrelations (figure 6.1) among children's characteristics. Among them the most interesting is that aptitude and socioeconomic status are not strongly associated. One would not, of course, expect to find substantial correlations

TABLE 6.5
CORRELATION MATRIX OF CHILDREN'S CHARACTERISTICS, INSTRUCTIONAL CONDITIONS, BASAL AND PHONICS LEARNING, AND FIRST GRADE ACHIEVEMENT (n = 147)

	1	2	3	4	5	6	7	8	9	10	11	12
1 Aptitude												
2 Socioeconomic Status	0.12											
3 Age	0.17	0.06										
4 Sex	0.16	0.06	-0.03									
5 Basal Group Size	0.30	-0.00	0.18	-0.03								
6 Group Mean Aptitude	0.79	0.13	0.15	0.19	0.38							
7 Basal Coverage	0.54	0.12	0.03	0.16	0.31	0.69						
8 Phonics Coverage	0.35	0.27	0.07	-0.01	0.42	0.44	0.51					
9 Basal Learning	0.59	0.11	0.05	0.16	0.34	0.72	0.93	0.50				
10 Phonics Learning	0.60	0.21	0.15	-0.02	0.45	0.65	0.51	0.62	0.60			
11 First Grade Achievement	0.70	0.19	0.15	0.20	0.38	0.77	0.75	0.57	0.83	0.76		
12 Second Grade Achievement	0.67	0.23	0.13	0.19	0.36	0.73	0.71	0.52	0.75	0.70	0.89	
Mean	37.9	2.1	74.1	0.5	12.8	37.9	228.7	46.3	190.0	19.7	0.0	0.0
Standard Deviation	18.8	0.9	3.9	0.5	7.1	14.8	100.0	15.8	105.6	13.5	1.9	1.9

Levels of significance: 0.05: $r > 0.17$; 0.01: $r > 0.23$.

with age and sex in coeducational classes containing a narrow age range of children.

The findings presented in figure 6.1 tell a clear and dramatic story. Teachers, in establishing the size of groups, take the aptitude of children into account; they appear to assign bright children to large groups, a finding consistent with our earlier analysis of group formation and change (chapter 4). While the relation between aptitude and group size is modest in magnitude (beta = 0.29), there is a very substantial relation between individual aptitude and the mean aptitude level of the groups to which individual children are assigned (beta = 0.72), indicating on the average that low aptitude children are placed in low groups, high aptitude children in high ones.

Most important in our attempt to disentangle the effects of aptitude and instruction on learning is the fact that the coverage of basal materials, a major instructional condition, is strongly related to group mean aptitude (beta = 0.65) and virtually unrelated to individual aptitude (beta = 0.01; from table 6.6). The mean aptitude of each group is established as an element of school production when reading groups are formed. The experiential side of this phenomenon is that children move more or less rapidly through their reading materials because teachers pace groups in accordance with the mean aptitude of each group. How much is covered, then, is derived from productive events occurring in the classroom, the assignment of children to groups, and not directly from how bright they are. Their brightness influences which group they are assigned to in the first place (as the teacher copes with the aptitude distribution of the class), and group assignment determines how fast they go, with all members of the same group going at the same pace.

It comes as no surprise, now, that children who cover a lot of basal material learn a lot of words (beta = 0.81); but more than that, how much they learn is again trivially related to their individual aptitudes (beta = 0.08; table 6.6). Aptitude enters the picture again only when we consider first grade reading achievement, a general standardized measure of vocabulary and comprehension. That is to say, it is the indication of general reading capacity (aptitude) that is associated with more general measures of learning, those not tied specifically to the curricular material in the basal reader, and evidently influenced by considerations extraneous to it. Moreover, the effect of aptitude on general first grade achievement (beta = 0.15) is smaller than that attributable to both basal (beta = 0.45) and phonics (beta = 0.31) learning. In other words, what the children have learned directly out of their basal reading materials has a greater impact on their general reading achievement than their aptitude, a finding that shows the predominance of instructional events and their immediate outcomes over aptitude on learning.

TABLE 6.6

BETA COEFFICIENTS SHOWING THE CONTRIBUTION OF CHILDREN'S BACKGROUND CHARACTERISTICS AND GROUP CONDITIONS TO SUCCESSIVE DEPENDENT VARIABLES (n = 147)

Independent Variables	Dependent Variables (Variable Numbers)						
	5	6	7	8	9	10	11[a]
1 Children's Aptitude	.29*	.72**	.01	−.01	.08	.20*	.15*
2 Children's SES	−.04	.04	.04	.22*	−.01	.07	.02
3 Children's Age (months)	.13	−.00	−.08	−.02	−.01	.02	.04
4 Children's Sex (m = 0; f = 1)	−.07	.08	.03	−.09	.00	−.11*	.09*
5 Basal Group Size		.17*	.07	.27*	.03	.11	−.01
6 Group Mean Aptitude			.65**	.09	.09	.24*	.08
7 Basal Coverage				.36*	.81**	−.48**	−.00
8 Phonics Coverage					.00	.35**	.06
9 Basal Words Learned						.56*	.45*
10 Phonics Learning							.31*
R	.34	.80	.69	.63	.93	.80	.91
R^2 (percent)	11	65	48	40	87	64	83
Adjusted R^2 (percent)	9	64	46	37	87	62	82
$\sqrt{1 - R^2}$	.94	.59	.72	.77	.36	.60	.41

[a] Measure of Standardized first grade reading achievement.

* Unstandardized coefficient is 2 to 4 times as large as the standard error.

** Unstandardized coefficient is 5 or more times as large as the standard error.

The phonics story is somewhat different and does not appear to be tied into the grouping process directly. Most interesting, however, is that *basal* coverage, not the characteristics of children, has the strongest impact on phonics coverage (beta = 0.36). This provides further evidence of the dependence of phonics upon basal instruction and suggests that the effects of grouping work indirectly through basal coverage. In addition, phonics coverage is influenced by group size, but this appears to reflect the unusual situation in school F, which had a heavy phonics program in classes that also had very large high groups—a finding more likely to be artifactual than real.

Several conditions influence phonics learning. Coverage has a moderately strong impact (beta = 0.35), but the most substantial influence is basal learning (beta = 0.56). Nevertheless, it may be improper to interpret basal learning as a causal influence because both kinds of learning occur together on an ongoing basis; rather, it is probably more appropriate to consider the two as being correlated.

The substantial negative path linking basal coverage and phonics learning (beta = −0.48) results from the inclusion of two very highly correlated conditions of this dependent variable, basal coverage and basal learning (r = 0.93; table 6.5). When we identify the contribution of basal coverage to phonics learning without including basal learning in the equation, the unstandardized coefficient (b) is −0.003 with a standard error of 0.01. That is, the two variables are virtually unrelated.

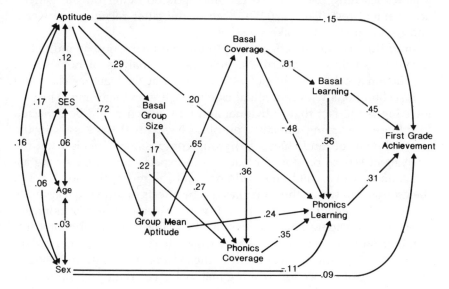

FIG. 6.1   Path analysis of children's characteristics, instructional conditions, and learning (n = 147).

When basal learning is then added to the equation, the contribution of basal coverage increases in magnitude substantially (b = −0.06) and the standard error doubles. At the same time, the standardized coefficient (beta) increases from −0.02 without basal learning in the equation to −0.48 with it included. This large negative path, then, we believe to be accounted for by the collinearity between the conditions influencing phonics learning; for that reason it is artifactual.

Grouping influences on phonics instruction are mostly indirect. This is in part because some phonics instruction takes place in whole class settings and also because phonics activities are derivative from basal instruction. Group mean aptitude, however, has a direct impact on phonics learning (beta = 0.24), a relation that we believe to indicate an aptitude climate characteristic of groups. Phonics learning is also influenced directly by individual aptitude (beta = 0.20), which raises the interesting question of why it influences phonics but not basal learning. As we explained earlier in this chapter, basal instruction is far richer; it takes more time and is more closely directed, supported, and supervised. By contrast, much of phonics instruction transpires with children working by themselves without much teacher engagement, with the result that the talents of the children must carry more of the burden in this sparse instructional atmosphere.

Finally, we find that phonics learning has a moderately strong impact on first grade reading achievement (beta = 0.31). Boys do better in phonics learning (beta = −0.11), and girls do better on the general achievement test (beta = 0.09). Both of the latter relations are weak, and we are unable to make sense of them.

In distinguishing the effects of aptitude and instruction on individual learning, we find a pattern that follows our analysis of how school production works, a sequence of relations that tie together class and group conditions with individual characteristics and learning. Most interesting is the fact that individual aptitude, which might be expected to influence learning directly, contributes with real force only in the establishment of (and change in) group composition. This is what the analysis of school production leads us to expect. We find a strong association between children's aptitudes and the mean aptitude level of the groups into which they are placed. The effects of individual aptitude are weak to negligible in connection with learning. What is more, instructional considerations take over as the major determinants of learning. In production terms, as we have shown in chapter 5, teachers adapt their activities to the mean aptitude of the groups they create and thereby establish a group pace for covering material. Accordingly, children who are members of high groups go quickly, those who are members of low groups go slowly, and their experiences of going quickly or slowly represent instructional conditions that determine how much they learn—not their individual aptitudes or their socioeconomic status.

Our attempt thus far to distinguish the effects of instruction and aptitude on learning has treated the whole sample of 147 cases. But we have reason to believe that the experiences of children might differ according to their aptitudes, and for that reason we partition our sample into segments of low, middle, and high aptitude to discover whether the generalizations we have drawn for all cases hold across the board or whether they are conditional.

Low Aptitude Children

Figure 6.2 presents a path analysis for the forty-five lowest aptitude children. Unexpectedly, no individual characteristics—including aptitude—have any effect on the elements of instruction, except for sex on phonics coverage, which we are hard put to explain. Most conspicuously and unlike the pattern in the full sample, individual aptitude is unrelated to group mean aptitude, a reflection of two considerations: first, the limited variation found in both individual and group mean aptitude; and second, the fact that children of low aptitude are assigned to low, middle, and high aptitude groups (a situation that contrasts with that of high aptitude children). Thus, even though low aptitude children are clustered more in low groups, group placement for them is to a certain extent independent of aptitude.

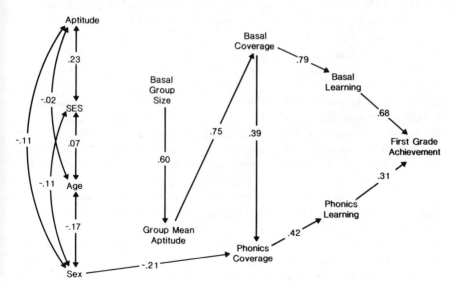

FIG. 6.2   Path analysis of children's characteristics, instructional conditions, and learning among low-aptitude children (n = 45).

Another finding that differs from the full sample analysis is that the size of the groups is much more strongly related to the mean aptitude of those groups. This appears to reflect the situation where high aptitude groups are larger than low aptitude groups, particularly in the spring. Accordingly, because low aptitude children are indeed assigned to all levels of groups, their group membership varies; and because the high groups are larger, we find this connection between group size and mean aptitude.

Otherwise, the story closely resembles that told for the entire sample: one set of linkages between group mean aptitude, basal coverage, basal words learned, and general achievement; and another set of linkages between phonics coverage, phonics learning, and general achievement—but with one major exception. In the low aptitude subsample, phonics learning is not related to basal learning, which indicates that among these children, who are the least ready to read, the acquisition of phonics skills does not occur derivatively from basal reading or in conjunction with it, but rather more narrowly reflects the pace of phonics instruction. In short, the low aptitude children learn the phonics they are taught and do not pick it up as a by-product of more general reading. (The correlation matrix and regression analysis appear in appendixes G and H.)

High Aptitude Children

Figure 6.3 shows the strong connection between the aptitudes of individual children and the mean aptitude of the instructional groups to which they are assigned—similar to what we found in the whole sample. This finding does not arise from the least talented of the high aptitude children being placed in low aptitude groups. Rather, all were placed in high groups, but the most talented were placed in high groups of higher mean aptitude while the less talented were placed in high groups of lower mean aptitude.

Socioeconomic status, which did not figure as an influence either in the whole sample or in the low aptitude portion of it, appears here to affect phonics coverage. We believe this reflects the greater stress placed on phonics instruction in the more well-to-do suburban schools. Age also appears for the first time, influencing phonics learning to a modest degree. We suspect that age represents an indication of maturity that makes it possible for the stronger readers to work by themselves on fairly demanding phonics activities. This interpretation is consistent with three other pieces of evidence. The first is that the older children among the ablest are placed in the largest groups, an indication that in group instruction they do not require the kind of close teacher direction needed by their younger compatriots. Group size, in turn, has a fairly substantial connection with phonics coverage. We do not consider the latter to be

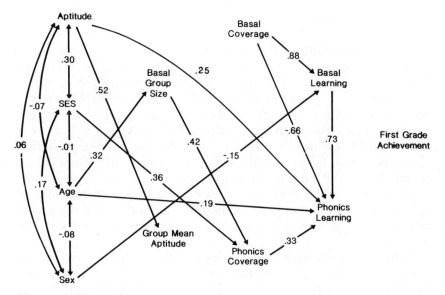

FIG. 6.3   Path analysis of children's characteristics, instructional conditions, and learning among high-aptitude children (n = 44).

a real finding, but simply a reflection of the fact that the most able children receive the most advanced instruction, which also takes place in large groups. Third, individual aptitude has a direct impact on phonics learning. Among the high aptitude children, then, we have a subplot consisting of loosely joined instructional and individual influences linked to phonics, an area of the reading curriculum emphasized among these children. Finally, sex is weakly related to basal learning (boys do better), and it is not clear why.

There is a major departure, however, from our findings based upon the total sample. The pace of basal instruction experienced by individual children is unrelated to the mean aptitude of the groups to which they belong (beta = 0.01). This finding, at least among high aptitude children, is an ostensible contradiction to the central argument that pace is determined by group mean aptitude. But the contradiction is only ostensible. In fact, while there is a strong overall connection in the total sample between group aptitude and basal pace (r = 0.69; table 6.6), there is at the same time very considerable variation in the pace at which high aptitude groups move through materials. In fact, we have found high groups of the same mean aptitude in different classes to proceed through materials at rates differing by a factor of more than two (table 5.1). At the individual level, then, some children in high aptitude groups move slowly, others quickly; and in chapter 5, we have already accounted for some of the variation in pace across groups similar in aptitude on the basis of the difficulty of instructional materials and the time allocated to reading.

The most dramatic finding, and one we referred to earlier, is that phonics learning is most strongly associated with basal learning (beta = 0.73). And while this finding appeared when we treated the whole sample, this present analysis shows it to be a phenomenon characteristic primarily of the high aptitude subsample. (It also appears, though not quite so strongly, among average aptitude children.) It suggests that one talent associated with high aptitude is the capacity to develop the skills of phonics analysis not only directly from phonics instruction but indirectly from basal story reading. The contrast with the lower aptitude children is striking, for they seem to learn primarily what they are taught and do not seem to bring any additional transformational capacity to their reading that permits them to derive phonics skills from basal instruction.

Perhaps the most significant departure of this path analysis from that based on the full sample is the apparent failure of either basal or phonics learning to influence general first grade achievement. In fact, no conditions, including individual characteristics, seem to influence general achievement. Perhaps perversely, we are not quite prepared to acknowledge that first grade reading achievement among high aptitude children goes unexplained, for several reasons. First, as appendix J shows, all conditions combined account for 70 percent of the variance, which is a substantial amount. Second, while the unstandardized regression coefficients are not twice their standard errors, they are very close to that. Third, coefficients for the relation of general achievement to both basal and phonics learning yield significant F ratios of 3.45 and 3.33 (d.f. 10, 33; $p < 0.01$), respectively. In sum, we believe it premature to conclude that the first grade reading achievement of high aptitude children is independent of the curricular learning shaped by rather potent instructional influences. (Appendix I contains the correlation matrix upon which the regression analysis in appendix J is based.)

We do not present the analysis of average aptitude children. It follows the same principles as the cases we have just considered, and although it contains some differences in particular findings, it poses no new interpretive issues.

SUMMARY

These analyses have demonstrated a chain of related events pertaining to the aptitudes of individual children, their group memberships, and the amount of material they cover that constitute the elements of their instructional experience and that strongly influence, in turn, both specific skill learning and general achievement. What we have really seen is a flattening out of our analysis of school production, the projection onto a one-dimensional (individual level) screen of a deeply layered set of events taking place at several organizational levels of the school system. Accordingly, when we show that individual aptitude is associated with membership in an instructional group of given mean aptitude, that association represents in silhouette the fact that teachers have sized up the aptitude distribution of the class and assigned children to instructional groups on the basis of that distribution. Their assignments to groups are based upon their aptitudes; so when we represent these productive events in classrooms at the individual level, we lose the depth but observe a relation between individual aptitude and the mean aptitude of each child's group.

Similarly, the association between the mean aptitude of a child's group and the pace of instruction does not really reflect two characteristics of the child but rather the fact that each individual in a group gets carried along at the pace of the group itself—a productive event that is characteristic of groups and only derivatively characteristic of the child by virtue of engagement in a group activity.

In general, the pace of instruction exerts the strongest influence on learning, a finding that holds solidly for basal word learning but less substantially for phonics learning. Curricular learning is the major influence on general achievement. Most interesting, of course, is the minor direct influence of individual aptitude on learning of any kind and its rather strong impact, not as an individual characteristic, but as a distributional property of a class on the shaping of instructional conditions— the arrangement of groups—that indirectly though powerfully affect learning. The basic outlines of the story stand up; they provide plausible support for contending that the aptitude–group–pace–learning sequence of events at the individual level parallels our analysis of the elements of school production.

7. Conclusion

One of the more interesting results of the publication of the Coleman report is that one of its major conclusions, that differences among schools are associated with small differences in students' achievement, has become part of the conventional wisdom. Some writers no longer consider it necessary either to confirm or to question this contention. For example, Graham refers to the documented ineffectiveness of schools "to overpower the influences of family, social class, and economic privilege in determining subsequent economic rewards" and also "in making children learn" (1980, pp. 123–24). We consider such taking of the evidence for granted to be lamentable because the conclusion is entirely premature. It stands only when we ignore the oft-repeated but rarely followed injunction to consider the nature and occurrence of events inside the schools, or when we think we have in fact considered those events but have only looked at the individual children who attend school.

We have argued in this book that those aspects of school organization and operation that have been commonly ignored or seriously misconceptualized are precisely the ones that show the greatest evidence of variation in their underlying conditions and outcomes; indeed, the greatest and most persuasive evidence that schools are actively productive

152

organizations has been left largely unexamined. To individualize schooling is to treat the school simply as an empty container in which we
observe how the characteristics of children and their experiences are
related to learning. It is to confuse the productive working of schools
with the attainments of children. The result of taking this perspective
is to put the nature of school and the organization of its productive
activities out of sight by construing the relevant evidence as pertaining
to individuals. By contrast, summarizing and comparing the properties
of the schools themselves average out and obscure from sight, though
by different means, this same organization of productive activities taking
place inside them—in classrooms and in instructional arrangements.

We have tried here to reopen the question of what educational effects
are and how they are produced, a question that has been rapidly falling
out of the realm of things problematic. In this pursuit, we find it useful
to distinguish what might be called school production from school productivity and, once that distinction has been drawn and its terms conceptualized, to investigate the connection between the two. School
production refers to matters of social and economic organization: to the
parts that constitute school systems, to the resources mobilized and
employed, and to the ways in which resources are put to use in the
various parts. The most fundamental problem is to identify what the
outcomes of the organization are, not simply the most salient one of
individual learning, but the variety of outcomes produced by different
parts of the school system, some of which have their primary impact
not directly on learning but on the operation of other parts of the system
itself.

The key to the analysis of production is the division of labor and the
allocation of resources to the various parts of the organization. School
systems are divided into distinct levels of organization—district, school,
class, group, and individual—each one of which has a particular and
characteristic productive agenda. The central problem, then, is to identify each agenda, to determine what takes place at each organizational
level and how it fits into the larger enterprise. We have designed this
book according to our sense of how districts, schools, classes, groups,
and individuals are linked together; each is characterized by a set of
activities with their ensuing outcomes, and the outcomes of one level
constitute productive conditions present at the next lower level. The
virtue of this formulation is that it identifies both the nature of production
at each level and how the levels are related to each other.

By denotation, production refers to an organization of activities. Accordingly, if school systems and their parts are to be compared to determine whether differences in production account for variations in
productivity, the comparisons must acknowledge the dynamic nature of
educational production—its active utilization of resources in variously

structured social arrangements. The standard analyses of educational production simply do not make comparisons among schools and among classes on the basis of the organization of their activities, according, that is, to how they work, but rather on the basis of the availability of resources. Even in cases where productivity *is* found to be related to differences among schools (Rutter et al. 1979) or to differences among classes (Bennett 1976), this contention is still true. The comparisons among school and class characteristics in these works are based upon static properties in the sense that they deal with whether an ad hoc but plausible collection of school characteristics (like time students spend on homework, library use, amount of teacher interaction with the whole class, public commendation of students for good work, and so on [Rutter et al. 1979, chapter 7]) or of class characteristics (like arrangements for individual or collective class activities, testing procedures, types of discipline, assignment of homework, and so on, combined to form indices of formal and informal classroom teaching [Bennett 1976, appendix A]) are related to student achievement. And while these works provide a far more optimistic picture than some other investigations of school and teacher effectiveness, they nevertheless provide little sense of the school or the class as operating enterprises, as going concerns, or of how schools and classes work as units of school organization. They convey little idea, moreover, of how the elements of production are combined in a coherent way, nor do they provide a general formulation of school production that gives conceptual coherence to the selection for investigation of certain properties of schools and classrooms and not others.

Our point of departure in investigating school production was the distributional properties of the different levels of school system organization. Beginning with the aptitude distribution in the whole sample of children, we observed whether the nature of the distribution changed as children in each district were sequentially assigned to schools, to classes, and to instructional groups. If the distribution between one level and the one immediately below it was the same, we presumed that an ordinary and routine assignment process was taking place. But when two adjacent distributions were markedly different, we felt we had presumptive evidence that something more than routine assignment was taking place by virtue of the fact that one distribution was being transformed into several smaller ones that had fundamentally different properties. Because the properties were so different, as between classes and instructional groups (but not between schools and classes), we believed that the events surrounding the distributional change indicated that something different was going to be done to the smaller aggregations of children for which the previous larger distributional arrangement would have been inappropriate. That is to say, whatever was going to happen to children in instructional groups, it was not only that the groups would be smaller than class size but also that the distribution of children in the smaller groups would have different social properties from those obtaining in the class.

This line of reasoning led us not simply to consider whether teachers grouped classes for instruction, but to identify the alternative ways in which they formed groups in response to the variety of aptitude distributions that characterized the several classes. This analysis uncovered the importance of the number of low aptitude children present in a class as representing an asymmetry in the instructional burden. The greater the burden, it turned out, the more constrained was the teacher in devising a workable grouping arrangement. In effect, teachers responded to the aptitude composition of their classes initially by creating different kinds of new social arrangements (instructional groups) and then, over the course of the year, by rearranging the pattern of groups depending on the workability of the initial plan: whether the groups were the right size and—we think—the right composition. These processes of group formation and change we consider to be productive activities.

The resulting group arrangements we regarded as classroom outcomes that had further relevance as instructional conditions at the group level. Indeed, it was only when we treated the instructional group as the unit of analysis that we began to make sense of the design of instruction. The amount of material covered by the members of instructional groups was primarily a function of group mean aptitude. In addition, the collinear effects of the conceptual difficulty of materials and the time allocated to certain instructional activities accounted for some observed differences in how much material groups of similar mean aptitude covered over the course of the year. Moreover, we identified classrooms where the mean aptitude of groups and the instructional materials would have permitted rapid coverage, but the groups nonetheless proceeded slowly. Thus, while enabling conditions are necessary, they may be insufficient to account for the differences in amount of material covered by groups; we suspect that teachers' preferences and their ability to employ the available instructional time usefully might account for some of the unexplained differences we observed.

Group properties and the instructional activities associated with them represent conditions that in turn influence individual learning. Although children are group members and class members, they experience instruction individually—they read the material assigned, receive help from the teacher, govern the proportion of available time they actually use for work, and learn. But to trace how group conditions bear on individual learning, it is necessary to understand the productive processes at the various levels of school systems. For example, instructional pace has a marked influence on individual learning, but it is inappropriate to think of pace as a condition that can be manipulated at the individual level. Rather, coverage is established for groups mainly in response to average group aptitude; accordingly, group recomposition may be required before a marked change in pace is possible. Further, coverage is responsive to the characteristics of materials and to the amount of time allocated to their use. For these reasons, it would be inappropriate to think of coverage as a condition that can be readily altered at the individual level because the availability of time and materials is influenced by events originating at the district, school, and class levels.

We have demonstrated that individual aptitude, which has been found to be a major correlate of learning, cannot be understood simply as a capacity having a direct bearing on learning. Rather, the collection of individual aptitudes taking the form of a class distribution was found to influence the formation of groups. Further, the average aptitude of instructional groups was shown (chapter 6) to exert more influence on the learning pace of children than their individual aptitudes. Indeed, as shown in chapter 3, the deviation of the individual aptitudes of children from the mean of their group accounted for little of the observed variation in their learning. We are dealing, then, not with a simple relation between independent and dependent variables, expressed by a statistic, but with a condition—children's aptitudes—to which forms of classroom organization and subsequent instructional activities constitute a set of responses. And while our analysis of learning proceeds at the individual level, it actually reflects a collective reality in which the distribution of aptitudes, as a class condition, gives rise to productive events that work themselves out at the class, group, and individual levels. It is a classroom condition, then, that sets the productive machinery of instruction in motion.

We are now able to provide a general characterization of what kind of phenomenon school production is and how it is related to productivity. We refer not so much to particular empirical relations as to kinds of relations. School production, first and foremost, has depth by virtue of the fact that it works across different levels of school system organization—a point we have perhaps belabored but that nevertheless requires great emphasis. Our approach, in effect, departs substantially from prevailing perspectives that flatten the elements of production by treating a single level of organization, the unfortunate by-product of seeking the one most appropriate level.

A corollary of treating production at several levels is that we can identify which events tend to be peculiar to each of them—that is, what aspects of the whole are the special province of districts, of schools, of classes, and of groups—and which occur at more than one level. When events are treated at the wrong level, when, for example, individual or class characteristics are expressed as properties of a school, the overall sense of what is going on becomes distorted. Things are believed to have an effect when they do not, or believed to have no effect when they actually have one.

Second, we have learned that not all relations between the elements of production can be treated as if they were independent forces exerting direct and immediate influences upon dependent outcomes. Viewing school production in this latter way creates optical illusions. Things are seen together in close contact when in fact their connections are indirect but nevertheless strong and important. We found it useful, therefore, to think about certain kinds of relations among the elements of production as concatenations of events that link contiguous levels of organization, that span them, or indeed that act directly upon each other within the same level. Part of the problem of understanding school production is to discover which influences work at close range and which work over longer spans.

Third, the findings tell us that we must not think about every condition as being continuous and linear or as standing alone in its impact. For example, the relation between how fast children proceed through their materials and how much they learn was, for the most part, linear in nature. Linear analysis, however, was inappropriate for examining the importance of differences in class size despite the fact that size is a variable that lends itself par excellence to linear measurement. And finally, we found that the characteristics of learning materials and the time allocated to instruction, in which materials are used in groups, varied simultaneously and—as far as we could tell—interconnectedly. We make no claim that no one else has discovered linear, nonlinear, and collinear relations; on the contrary. We do claim, however, that the last two have too often been collapsed into linear form. And perhaps more important, we claim that knowledge of these different kinds of associations has too seldom been used to characterize the different kinds of events occurring in different locations of school system organization. Not all collinear relations, in other words, should be treated as errors necessitating the separation of joint effects. There are times when collinearity describes reality quite correctly.

And fourth, we have been impressed with the fact that school production is composed of constraining and permissive conditions that turn out to be problematic for teachers in two ways. First, there are difficult conditions—such as a large number of low aptitude children—that reduce the available alternatives for action sometimes to unsatisfactory ones. Second, there are situations that permit more choices but where the choices are generally encumbered. Thus, decisions about the use of materials entail joint decisions about the use of time. It is these problematic conditions that make nonlinear and collinear conditions so important to the analysis of school production.

While our findings illuminate the nature of school production and its relation to productivity in both descriptive and analytical ways, they also represent the results of an approach to investigating certain broader educational issues that contrast with more traditional ways of looking at them. There are three issues in particular that our work places in uncustomary light, issues closely tied up with problems of educational production but that also have been subjects of controversial public debate. These are the problems of class size, of ability grouping, and of equal educational opportunity.

CLASS SIZE

The size of collective aggregates has proved problematic not only for students of school organization, but also for those studying all sorts of organizations and their parts (Scott 1975). One trouble with size (the number of people who are members of groups) is that it is too easy to measure. Because heads can be counted so readily, and as a result groupings so easily compared according to the size of their membership, there is an insidious impulse to think about size, both in general and as it pertains to school classes, as if it were necessarily a continuous variable in one dimension.

Size has also been treated in research on educational production as a static property that could be varied quantitatively but without much thought given to its conceptualization. The inconclusiveness of findings, however, about the relation between class size and learning has recently spawned a new line of research in which the results of myriad investigations are brought together and reanalyzed with new statistical techniques to determine whether there actually are important and systematic implications of class size hiding behind the methodological inadequacies of many of the studies. Glass and Smith, by employing these newer techniques, were able to show that differences in achievement are greatest in a range of class sizes between ten and twenty, particularly in well-controlled studies in which children are randomly assigned to classes (1978, pp. 45–46). And while this may be true, it is difficult to understand why, unless one recognizes that this work does not deal in conceptual terms with class characteristics generally and with size in particular. Only size as a numerical property—number of children—is subjected to statistical analysis.

While we do not gainsay the value of codifying a large and amorphous body of hitherto inconclusive information, we nevertheless do not believe that codification is necessarily the best way to recast a troublesome and mystifying set of findings. There is ample evidence not simply that the size of groupings is a quantitative matter but that it has qualitative and structural meanings as well (Lipset, Trow, and Coleman 1956, chapter 9; Simmel 1950). Our own findings, moreover, provide clear evidence that size needs to be thought about in more than numerical terms and that accordingly a conceptual assessment rather than a quantitative reanalysis seems to be the better initial alternative.

Our analysis indicates that class size should be treated, along with several other class properties, as a prevailing condition that proves to be problematic for teachers, that they must take into account when they organize children for instruction. In our smallest classes, with from ten to fifteen fewer members than the largest, teachers attempted to instruct the class as a whole for several months; in the larger classes, grouping began at the start of the school year. It might have been size alone that made it possible to delay grouping; it might also have been that the smallest classes had the smallest number of low aptitude children. Neither the average level of aptitude nor its dispersion was a relevant consideration because in these respects the small classes resembled some of the larger ones. In short, we have evidence, though less than conclusive, that class size acts as a constraint on early alternative grouping arrangements. Of course, we do not know whether teachers of small classes would have grouped at the start of school if there had been a substantial number of low aptitude children.

In the larger classes, it is not the size of the class per se that is important for the organization of instruction but the size of the low aptitude contingent of children. Whether there are few or many such children sets constraints on how teachers establish instructional groups, in particular the size configuration of groups. A large contingent means a large low group and accordingly a class configuration of equal sized groups. A small contingent allows the teachers leeway in determining how large the groups will be; it is a less constraining condition. Class size, moreover, must not be treated as a condition in isolation from other class properties. Its importance for instructional organization lies in its association with the distribution of aptitudes.

Class size together with the class aptitude distribution has instructional implications for how teachers form groups because the way in which groups are formed influences the distribution of aptitudes among groups. It is unfortunate, of course, that our data do not permit us to examine the internal structure of groups because we conjecture that their internal diversity, which may well be related to group size, represents a constraint on how much material gets covered. Nevertheless, the mean aptitude of each group is established through the process of group formation. It is established by teachers not as a deliberate attempt to create groups of given mean aptitude, but as part of the process of coming to terms with the overall composition of the class.

It should be evident by now that we have intentionally avoided considering the direct connection between class size and achievement (in contrast to Glass and Smith as well as many others) because we do not believe size as an isolated numerical property has any such connection. Nor do we think it appropriate to treat it as we would some other continuous variable in a conventional conditional analysis. Rather, it should be regarded as an indication of a problematic situation (which comprises other conditions as well—most notably the class aptitude distribution) to which teachers respond with a small number of instructional solutions. Indeed, we would not expect to find direct connections between class size and learning for two reasons. First, the world of school classrooms does not seem to work that way. As our discussion indicates, a complex chain of conditions intervenes between class size and learning so that any analysis that presumes a direct and simple relation between size and learning is bound to be off the mark. Second, along the chain of prevailing conditions, not all associations among productive elements are linear. The statistical equations by which one relates size to learning, when pressed to include the variety of qualitative elements entailed, do not readily accommodate conditional relations of the sort described when multiple solutions to the same problem are possible. Moreover, while teachers often believe that the size of their classes is the origin of their instructional burdens, it may not simply be size but other conditions that might or might not be generally associated with it, such as the number of difficult or unprepared children. Thus, a class of twenty-five with ten hard to teach or hard to manage children might be no easier than a class of thirty with the same number of tough customers.

In effect, class size appears to be a condition that constrains the number of different kinds of instructional arrangements a teacher can fashion, with teachers having more choices when classes are small. There is no reason to assume, however, that because choices may be few, the alternatives are also unworkable. Size does not, however, shape instructional conditions directly as indicated by the fact that it is essentially unrelated to the major instructional condition influencing learning: namely, the coverage of material. It comes as no surprise, then, that size by itself should all along be found to have an inconsistent relation to achievement. And at the lower end of the size ten to twenty range where Glass and Smith found their most marked effects, one simply does not find very many real public elementary school classes.

ABILITY GROUPING

The forms of ability grouping used in American schools include the establishment of separate academic and vocational schools, the tracking of students into college preparatory and other secondary school curricula, their assignment into homogeneously composed classes and into instructional groups within classes. The body of research that purports to investigate grouping is utterly confused for at least three reasons. First, one finds a lack of caution in keeping ideological preference distinct from analysis as well as a related failure to distinguish the existence of groups from the uses to which they are put. Second, there is no comprehensive formulation of grouping in school systems, with the result that different types of grouping become confounded. Typically, only one type is investigated at a time, with the ensuing failure to account for other methods of reducing diversity among students. Finally, the consequences of ability grouping are sought in remote indices of effectiveness, such as individual achievement, rather than in systematic analyses of the consequences of school level grouping which yields classes of varying composition which in turn influences grouping within classes and subsequently instructional design and individual learning.

The rationale for grouping has historically taken two forms. First, it has been considered a mechanism for reducing diversity in student characteristics in both schools and classes. Second, it has been considered a means for individualizing instruction, for doing what is pedagogically appropriate for each child. This latter aim is clearly expressed in a 1928 manual on reading instruction, cited by Smith, that advocated the use of ability groups within classes, a practice that had become widespread in the 1920s: "The pupils in any third grade should be divided into about three groups according to their reading abilities and each group should be permitted to progress as rapidly as its ability will allow. In this way the teacher's instruction can be adapted to meet the needs of the accelerated or fast group who learn with little or no difficulty; of the middle group . . . and of the slow group" (1965, p. 240). And while reducing diversity has often been considered dangerous because it provides opportunities for improperly classifying and stereotyping students, individualizing has generally been taken to be a "good thing." As Findley and Bryan comment, grouping within classes, or individualizing instruction, is "an accepted and commended practice" (1970, p. 2), while grouping into classes brings about undesirable consequences especially for members of minority groups and those coming from poor socioeconomic circumstances. But in reality, reducing diversity and individualizing are frequently different names for the same thing, and one need only keep straight the organizational level at which the distribution of students is rearranged.

Yet it is not altogether clear why the grouping of classes has such evil consequences while grouping within them is believed to be instructionally sound. What is to prevent assigning disadvantaged children to the lowest groups, treating them badly in the bargain, and perpetuating their already straitened circumstances? Indeed that is precisely the result that Rist (1970) anticipates and describes in his study of a single case— the use of grouping to fulfill teachers' prophesies of who will succeed and who will fail—though why teachers make such prophesies in the first place is not in the least bit obvious. Moreover, the fact that demonstrably slower students, whatever their social background, are assigned to low groups does not by itself indicate the fulfillment of illegitimate prophesies. Indeed, there may be instructional benefits that accrue: such children may learn better if they are not paced too quickly or given materials that are too advanced. Deleterious consequences do occur, however, when children able to move quickly are held back and when those who would benefit from more gradual instruction are brought along too quickly.

All forms of grouping are the object of ambivalent and conflicting sentiments which, we believe, are largely explained by the imposition of ideological and instructional preferences onto a body of poorly formulated and empirically inconclusive research. The majority of investigations have focused on the school level grouping of students into classes by ability and in point of fact have examined the resulting influence of class composition (not of grouping) on achievement (Goldberg, Passow, and Justman 1966; Borg 1965). Typically, studies of school grouping do not inquire about further ability grouping occurring within classes though such further differentiation may actually confound the results of comparisons across classrooms by ignoring their internal variation. The fundamental difficulty with studies that relate class composition directly either to the mean achievement of a class or to that of individuals is that they ignore elements of instructional organization. Further, they overlook the connections between classroom properties and those of groups established within classes. A notable exception to this tendency is found in the work of Hallinan and Sørenson (1981), who treat group characteristics both in their own right and in connection with class composition.

Summers (1979), one of the few investigators who does take groups explicitly into account, treated both the composition of classes and their division into instructional groups of different sizes. She found that children in classes containing both small and large groups do better than those in classes that provide only individual and small group instruction. But which groups are large and small, and what kinds of children are assigned to each? Under what circumstances do teachers establish large and small groups, in what combinations, and in what order over the course of a school year? A formulation such as Summers's, based upon the individual grouping experiences of children together with such class characteristics as composition and whether groups of different sizes are present, cannot explore the question of how classroom instruction is organized. This is because the groups themselves and the classrooms that give rise to them are not the subject of inquiry.

Groups are organizational forms designed for instructional activities not readily carried out in the whole class. Our findings show that teachers both form *and then use* groups instructionally in different ways. Their different uses appear most clearly in our evidence that *similarly* composed groups are not necessarily treated alike: some high groups proceed more than two times as rapidly as other high groups, and some low groups proceed about three times as rapidly as other low groups, with very substantial associated differences in learning. One might refer to these patterns of findings as evidence of inequality of opportunity. One might also refer to them as evidence of variation in teachers' instructional preferences as they pertain to the importance of coverage and mastery. It is also possible that other group characteristics besides mean aptitude (such as dispersion and skewness, properties we were unable to measure) and other individual characteristics besides aptitude (such as social maturity and attentiveness) might explain group generated differences in coverage and learning.

What, then, of the harmful social consequences of grouping? In the same way that the instructional use of groups varies, their social use can also vary. The fact of grouping affords overtly and covertly biased teachers opportunities to perpetuate inequalities of circumstance associated with race, ethnicity, and socioeconomic status; but it is difficult to see how it increases the opportunities for such malevolence over and above those present when other kinds of instructional arrangements are employed, including heterogeneous whole class instruction. Moreover, when classes are grouped internally for reading, children spend only a fraction of the day in groups. One would be hard-pressed to argue that these group experiences far overwhelm children's experience in ungrouped classroom situations, which indeed preempt a larger proportion of the school day.

At the same time, grouping arrangements do provide opportunities for teachers to deal with the problems of slow learners; and as our evidence shows, teachers use a lengthened school day to provide additional *grouped* phonics instruction, particularly beneficial for low aptitude children. Yet there is nothing in the phenomenon of grouping that guarantees its salutary instructional use. We find additional evidence that teachers both change the nature of grouping arrangements and transfer children from group to group depending on the workability of the prior arrangement and on the progress of the children. At least in these schools, the evidence shows that grouping arrangements are not used rigidly, while no doubt other studies might find teachers who use groups to express their prejudices or fulfill their social prophesies.

The phenomenon of instructional grouping, most prevalent in the lowest elementary school grades, is part of the social organization of production in school systems. There are, of course, means by which teachers manage the problems posed by diversity in the higher grades that this study did not address. Most important in this discussion, however, is the fact that the uses of instructional grouping are multiple, and its contribution to learning lies in its use and not simply in its existence. There is little in our evidence to support tendentious conclusions that grouping in the nature of the case perpetuates social inequality or that its consequences are otherwise vicious.

EQUALITY OF OPPORTUNITY

A perennial issue in understanding the relation between education and society is whether schools are social agencies that perpetuate distinctions based upon family background, that drive a wedge between background and adult status so that they become independent of each other, or that equalize status distinctions or the conditions on which they are founded. To believe that schools either can or should do the last of these requires a faith that they have a greater influence than socioeconomic background in determining future life-chances. For several decades debates have raged in this and other countries over the relative influences of education and social class.

In what has become a familiar observation about the efficacy of schooling, Jencks et al. comment as follows: "It is true that schools have 'inputs' and 'outputs,' and that one of their nominal purposes is to take human 'raw materials' (i.e., children) and convert it into something more 'valuable' (i.e., employable adults). Our research suggests, however, that the character of a school's output depends largely on a single input, namely the characteristics of the entering children. Everything else—the school budget, its policies, the characteristics of the teachers—is either secondary or completely irrelevant" (1972, p. 256). It would seem that this contention and our findings contradict each other—to say the least. They do in the sense that we have found school conditions in the category of "everything else" that exert powerful influences on learning. At the same time, one should be aware that Jencks et al. and we are addressing entirely different questions that only appear on the surface—and because of superficialities in the use of language—to be alike.

Jencks and his colleagues were concerned with whether the amount and quality of schooling obtained by different individuals would make them more equal in status when they became adults. This is not the same question as how schools work to produce what they do. And while Jencks and his colleagues are no doubt correct that schools are not the great equalizer, their conclusions about the ineffectuality of budget, policy, and teachers are gratuitous in the extreme because the research they review and reanalyze simply does not deal directly or adequately with those considerations. In particular, it has consistently ignored the alternative uses to which budgetary allocations are put as well as the instructional activities of teachers. In that research, questions about budget, policy, teachers, and other school resources are actually treated as aspects of students' individual experiences. The standard technique for determining the effects of schooling has been to consider whether individuals' achievement (or status) is determined by their attendance at schools with different budgets, policies, and teacher characteristics. But in many investigations, teacher characteristics and other class and school properties are not those actually experienced by individual students but rather the averaged values of school and district properties applied to all children in a school. Furthermore, the properties of any given school, despite the fact that they affect the individual members of the student body in different ways, are assigned equally to each student. As a result, the different ways that a school affects the different individuals who attend it are obliterated or simply never examined for their influence on achievement. Under these circumstances, it is no surprise that the socioeconomic background of individuals turns out to be the major determinant of their achievement.

The traditional methodological technique of assigning the properties of each school (or class) to all students who attend it, or—what amounts to the same thing—of comparing the averaged characteristics of schools or classes, removes the possibility of finding out whether what happens organizationally inside the school varies and then influences achievement. For these reasons, we have taken special care to examine the internal workings of school and classroom organization. For if it turns out—as indeed it does—that the experiences of children vary enormously within schools, and even within classes, then we must rethink what have become standard and conventional conclusions about equality of opportunity.

One of our more interesting findings speaks directly to the point (appendix C and table 5.1). School B is an inner city black school. Among its four first grade classes were five instructional groups whose mean aptitudes ranged narrowly from twenty-eight to thirty-three. Yet, among those five groups, the pace of instruction varied from ninety-three words covered over the year to three hundred twenty-four words. School D is suburban and white. It contained two groups that moved at the same rapid pace—three hundred forty-seven words. Yet the mean aptitude levels of the two groups were forty-one and seventy, a very large difference. These disjunctions between group aptitude and instructional pace, moreover, are found not only within the same school but within the same class. As we noted earlier, the teachers in school C subscribed strongly to egalitarian beliefs; and presumably as a result of that we find similarities in instructional pace; yet these similarities in coverage were combined with differences in aptitude as large as thirty points. And we know, of course, that children's coverage of material, determined by their group membership, has very substantial effects on how much they learn.

It must be obvious from these findings that within the same school and even within the same class, low aptitude children who happen to be placed in high aptitude groups are given more words to learn and as a result learn more than equally talented peers who are paced more slowly; and by the same token, some very able children are paced much too slowly and do not learn nearly as much as their equally talented compatriots. The magnitude of the differences in coverage and learning, moreover, is very substantial. It must be equally obvious that taking the characteristics of the school as the basis for determining the equality of children's educational experiences is hopelessly inadequate. Within each school, the differences in children's opportunities to learn are very great. In addition, differences in opportunity occur *within* both predominantly black and predominantly white schools; the racial composition of these schools, therefore, is not a major determinant of the instructional condition—coverage—that contributes so substantially to learning.

In contrast to our interest in first grade reading as an indication of achievement, Jencks and his colleagues were concerned with adult status as a product of schooling. These two achievements are markedly different; and furthermore, not much if anything is known about the long sequential processes by which school learning, through the grades, through college, and through the early stages of a work career, contribute to later adult achievements. Moreover, it is difficult to imagine how specific school achievements can be anything more than one among a number of conditions that influence adult earnings and occupational status at mid-life. Nevertheless, if such achievements are not necessarily very large or direct influences upon adult status, there is an important civic sense in which they represent basic and general skills out of which later achievements can be fashioned. It is our contention that forming this foundation of basic skills has much more to do with questions of equality than whether there is a direct association between amount of schooling and adult status, which ignores the range of contingencies that affect people's careers from the time they complete school to the prime of their working lives.

Our evidence indicates that vast inequalities in educational experience—at least in first grade reading—exist inside schools and, to a lesser but by no means trivial degree, inside classrooms. They are associated with grouping, but more importantly with the differences in instruction applied to groups, even to groups that resemble each other in composition. Whether these inequalities also constitute inequities is a separate matter. Moreover, the inequalities appear to be of much smaller magnitude between schools. One implication of this evidence is that for those who are concerned with improved instruction and improved levels of learning, public policies that simply reshuffle children from school to school or that promise free choice of school are rather wide of the mark.

They are premised on the assumption that it is school differences per se that will change the character of children's educational experiences. We find by contrast that it is the differences within schools that must be contended with, and moreover that we know what some of these differences are, how they get there, and what they mean. Note, however, that this is a distinctly different, though not unrelated, question from that of civil rights. The balancing of school populations insofar as it pertains to equal access to public facilities is a legal question bearing on the rights of citizenship. The solution to this problem is not necessarily coincident with the solution to the problem of instructional efficacy and school production.

*   *   *

We have tried in these pages to show that in the analysis of schooling it is important to recognize the difference between the workings of schools, the nature and magnitude of their effects, and the connection between the two. We have also tried to show that a formulation of how schools work has implications for how one thinks about several issues of current educational policy. It should not go unnoticed, moreover, that both the formulation and the empirical work contributing to it represent a departure from current views about the nature of teaching.

Our argument states that teaching is an activity that is basically a collective enterprise even though it is designed to produce learning in individual children. In classroom settings teachers deal with children in collective arrangements. We can reveal the nature of teaching by discovering the properties of the initial collective arrangement the teacher confronts—the distributive characteristics of the class and the resources made available by the administration—the constraints it imposes, and the alternative courses of action that become possible in light of those constraints. These alternative courses of action constitute the various ways teachers transform the class into social arrangements that are more or less conducive to instruction and, once those arrangements have been established, use available resources—time, materials, children's characteristics, and their own talents—in alternative ways. These questions of alternative social arrangements and alternative employment of resources represent the problematics of teaching. Their substantive categories have been identified in the body of this book.

Appendixes

APPENDIX A
SIZE AND APTITUDE DISTRIBUTIONS OF DISTRICTS AND SCHOOLS

District	School	Estimated Actual Size	Sample Size	Children's Aptitudes		
				Mean	Standard Deviation	Skewness
I	A, B	—[a]	62	34.13	17.61	0.63
II	C, D	—	39	38.90	19.60	0.52
III	E, F	—	46	42.04	19.11	0.19
I	A	111[b]	17	40.47	21.34	−0.06
	B	136	45	31.73	15.58	0.91
II	C	59	19	41.32	16.34	0.63
	D	54	20	36.60	22.44	0.66
III	E	57	16	39.75	19.14	0.53
	F	106	30	43.27	19.31	0.04

[a] District sizes cannot be estimated from our data.

[b] We sampled only one class from school A (class 01). We know, however, that school A had three classes of equal size (n = 37).

APPENDIX B
SIZE AND APTITUDE DISTRIBUTIONS OF BASAL INSTRUCTIONAL GROUPS (FALL)

District	School	Class	Instructional Group	Estimated Actual Size	Sample Size	Mean Aptitude
I	A	01	Low	9	4	19.50
			Mid	13	6	30.83
			High	15	7	60.71
	B	02	Low	11	4	18.00
			Mid	13	5	28.00
			High	11	4	30.00
		03	Low	4	2	14.50
			Mid	14	7	28.00
			High	18	9	48.89
		04	Mid	5	2	22.00
			High	10	4	37.75
		05	Low	13	3	16.33
			Mid	13	3	24.67
			High	9	2	56.50
II	C	06	Mid_1	10	3	26.33
			Mid_2	10	3	41.67
		07	Mid	20	6	46.17
		08	Mid	19	7	43.43
	D	09	Low	2	1	20.00
			Mid	11	5	20.80
			High	14	6	51.17
		10	Low	10	3	18.67
			Mid	7	2	17.50
			High	10	3	70.00
III	E	11	Low	4	1	25.00
			Mid	16	4	37.50
			High	8	2	46.50
		12	Low	16	5	24.04
			High	13	4	61.50
	F	13	Low	9	2	20.50
			High	28	6	64.33
		14	Low	2	1	19.00
			Mid	5	2	34.50
			High	26	11	48.18
		15	Mid	36	8	31.62

APPENDIX C

SIZE AND APTITUDE DISTRIBUTIONS OF BASAL INSTRUCTIONAL GROUPS (SPRING)

District	School	Class	Instructional Group	Estimated Actual Size	Sample Size	Mean Aptitude
I	A	01	Low	9	4	19.50
			Mid	4	2	20.00
			High	24	11	51.82
	B	02	Low	5	2	15.50
			Low-Mid	8	3	23.00
			Mid	11	4	28.00
			High	11	4	30.00
		03	Low	4	2	14.50
			Mid	8	4	28.75
			Mid-High	10	5	33.00
			High	14	7	50.86
		04	Mid	10	4	28.25
			High	5	2	41.00
		05	Low	13	3	16.33
			Mid	9	2	26.00
			High	13	3	45.00
II	C	06	Mid_1	10	3	26.33
			Mid_2	10	3	41.67
		07	Mid_1	10	3	30.67
			Mid_2	10	3	61.67
		08	Mid_1	11	4	40.75
			Mid_2	8	3	47.00
	D	09	Low	2	1	20.00
			Mid	4	2	21.00
			High	21	9	41.00
		10	Low	7	2	20.00
			Low-Mid	7	2	17.50
			Mid	3	1	16.00
			High	10	3	70.00
III	E	11	Low	4	1	25.00
			Mid	8	2	23.50
			Mid-High	8	2	39.00
			High	8	2	59.00
		12	Low	13	4	25.25
			Mid	10	3	42.33
			High	6	2	70.00
	F	13	Low	9	2	20.50
			High	28	6	65.83
		14	Low	3	1	19.00
			Mid	15	5	47.60
			High	15	5	52.20
		15	Low-Mid	10	3	34.00
			Mid	26	8	30.25

APPENDIX D
FREQUENCY DISTRIBUTION OF APTITUDE SCORES

Aptitude	Score	Frequency
Low	05–06	1
(n = 45)	07–08	0
	09–10	0
	11–12	1
	13–14	5
	15–16	7
	17–18	4
	19–20	15
	21–22	11
	23–24	1
Average	25–26	11
(n = 58)	27–28	6
	29–30	4
	31–32	9
	33–34	6
	35–36	1
	37–38	6
	39–40	2
	41–42	2
	43–44	1
	45–46	7
	47–48	3
High	49–50	1
(n = 44)	51–52	1
	53–54	6
	55–56	2
	57–58	2
	59–60	4
	61–62	3
	63–64	4
	65–66	1
	67–68	4
	69–70	16
Cutting Points:	24	0
	49	0

APPENDIX E

CALCULATION OF INDICES OF GROUP CONFIGURATION

1. Number of Groups: Reported by teachers of each class in December and May of first grade.
2. Size Inequality: Calculated from the average of deviations of the actual size of groups from the average group size. For example, class 01 contained three groups with 9, 13, and 15 members and had an average group size of 12.3. The deviations of 3.3, 0.7, and 2.7 yield an average deviation of 2.2.
3. Discreteness: Calculated by the intraclass correlation for each class, which provides a description of the aptitude heterogeneity of individuals in groups compared with total class variation in aptitude. The intraclass correlation (R) is estimated by:

$$R = \frac{MSB - MSW}{MSB + (n-1)MSW},$$

where MSB and MSW are the mean squares between and within groups (error), where

$$n = \frac{1}{G-1}\left[\sum_{g=1}^{G} n_g - \frac{\sum_{g=1}^{G} n_g^2}{\sum_{g=1}^{G} n_g}\right],$$

and where G = number of groups, n_g = number of individuals per group ($g = 1 \ldots G$). Although the theoretical minimum and maximum of this index are zero and one, we found two negative values. These values can be negative, however, if MSW is greater than MSB. This indeed was the case in two classes.
4. Group Range: Differences among groups in a class were estimated by taking the range among groups in mean aptitude. For example, class 01 contained top and bottom groups with mean aptitude scores of 60.71 and 19.50, respectively, on the Word Learning Tasks. The range for that class, then, was 41.21 in the fall (figures shown in appendixes B and C).

APPENDIX F

Correlation Matrix of Instructional Conditions, Class and Group Properties, and Basal and Phonics Learning (n = 147)

	1	2	3	4	5	6	7	8	9	10	11	12	13	14	15	16	17
1 Basal Learning																	
2 Phonics Learning	0.60																
3 Basal Coverage	0.93	0.51															
4 Phonics Coverage	0.50	0.62	0.51														
5 Basal Supervision	0.10	−0.06	0.14	−0.14													
6 Phonics Supervision	0.12	0.49	0.07	0.57	−0.32												
7 Basal Instruct. Time	0.32	0.41	0.35	0.57	0.34	0.44											
8 Phonics Instruct. Time	0.18	0.51	0.15	0.68	−0.34	0.78	0.41										
9 Total Reading Time	0.43	0.39	0.44	0.52	0.23	0.32	0.84	0.54									
10 Basal Mater. Diff.	0.29	0.23	0.33	0.47	−0.03	0.16	0.67	0.41	0.83								
11 Phonics Mater. Diff.	0.21	0.50	0.23	0.75	−0.18	0.71	0.73	0.86	0.73	0.71							
12 Teacher Experience	0.15	−0.26	0.19	−0.06	0.47	−0.29	−0.06	−0.39	−0.14	−0.33	−0.44						
13 Length of Day	0.12	0.54	0.09	0.48	0.09	0.60	0.74	0.65	0.66	0.51	0.80	−0.59					
14 Basal Group Size	0.34	0.45	0.31	0.42	−0.32	0.37	−0.03	0.43	0.02	−0.11	0.23	−0.19	0.16				
15 Phonics Group Size	0.00	−0.25	0.06	−0.05	−0.03	−0.32	−0.45	−0.48	−0.65	−0.49	−0.51	0.55	−0.72	0.21			
16 Class Size	−0.14	−0.23	−0.15	−0.27	0.03	−0.14	−0.65	−0.19	−0.68	−0.83	−0.55	0.48	−0.60	0.27	0.60		
17 Number Low Aptitude	−0.27	−0.32	−0.23	−0.24	−0.17	−0.35	−0.68	−0.15	−0.59	−0.29	−0.31	0.02	−0.49	0.09	0.50	0.55	
Mean	190.0	19.7	228.7	46.3	32.3	6.9	44.0	28.2	122.4	332.5	54.2	4.6	5.4	12.8	20.7	31.3	9.9
Standard Deviation	105.6	13.5	100.0	15.8	10.7	8.7	14.9	11.7	20.0	14.2	9.9	5.9	0.1	7.1	11.4	5.7	5.6

Levels of significance: 0.05: r > 0.17; 0.01: r > 0.23.

APPENDIX G
Correlation Matrix of Children's Characteristics, Instructional Conditions, Basal and Phonics Learning, and First Grade Achievement among Low Aptitude Children (n=45)

	1	2	3	4	5	6	7	8	9	10	11	12
1 Aptitude												
2 Socioeconomic Status	0.23											
3 Age	−0.02	0.07										
4 Sex	−0.11	−0.11	−0.17									
5 Basal Group Size	0.25	0.13	−0.06	−0.19								
6 Group Mean Aptitude	0.35	0.05	−0.05	−0.03	0.62							
7 Basal Coverage	0.27	0.13	0.02	−0.12	0.44	0.71						
8 Phonics Coverage	0.22	0.35	−0.02	−0.31	0.41	0.34	0.47					
9 Basal Learning	0.21	0.06	0.04	−0.05	0.42	0.70	0.87	0.37				
10 Phonics Learning	0.15	0.22	0.07	−0.19	0.53	0.45	0.47	0.60	0.47			
11 First Grade Achievement	0.30	0.18	0.06	−0.04	0.47	0.59	0.75	0.49	0.82	0.66		
12 Second Grade Achievement	0.33	0.28	0.13	−0.04	0.47	0.58	0.66	0.42	0.69	0.60	0.84	
Mean	18.2	2.0	72.9	0.4	10.9	25.6	161.6	41.2	114.5	11.9	−1.5	−1.4
Standard Deviation	3.5	0.8	3.7	0.5	6.7	9.3	93.3	15.8	88.9	11.7	1.5	1.5

Levels of significance: 0.05: $r > 0.30$; 0.01: $r > 0.39$.

APPENDIX H

BETA COEFFICIENTS SHOWING THE CONTRIBUTION OF CHILDREN'S BACKGROUND CHARACTERISTICS AND GROUP CONDITIONS TO SUCCESSIVE DEPENDENT VARIABLES AMONG LOW APTITUDE CHILDREN (n = 45)

Independent Variables	Dependent Variables (Variable Numbers)						
	5	6	7	8	9	10	11[a]
1 Children's Aptitude	.21	.23	-.01	.02	-.04	-.06	.13
2 Children's SES	.06	-.07	.09	.26	-.03	.05	.03
3 Children's Age (months)	-.09	.01	.03	-.07	.04	.10	.03
4 Children's Sex (m=0, f=1)	-.18	.11	-.10	-.21*	.03	.01	.10
5 Group Size		.60*	-.06	.22	.01	.29	.06
6 Group Mean Aptitude			.75**	-.10	.16	.04	-.15
7 Basal Coverage				.39*	.79**	-.12	.03
8 Phonics Coverage					-.03	.42*	.06
9 Basal Learning						.28	.68**
10 Phonics Learning							.31*
R	.31	.67	.47	.63	.89	.71	.89
R² (percent)	10	44	22	40	78	51	80
Adjusted R² (percent)	1	37	12	29	74	38	74
$\sqrt{1 - R^2}$	.95	.75	.88	.77	.47	.70	.45

a   Measure of standardized first grade reading achievement.

*   Unstandardized coefficient is 2 to 4 times as large as the standard error.

**   Unstandardized coefficient is 5 or more times as large as the standard error.

APPENDIX I

Correlation Matrix of Children's Characteristics, Instructional Conditions, Basal and Phonics Learning, and First Grade Achievement among High Aptitude Children (n = 44)

	1	2	3	4	5	6	7	8	9	10	11	12
1 Aptitude												
2 Socioeconomic status	0.30											
3 Age	-0.07	-0.01										
4 Sex	0.06	0.17	-0.08									
5 Basal Group Size	0.10	-0.14	0.32	-0.17								
6 Group Mean Aptitude	0.54	0.26	0.20	0.23	0.11							
7 Basal Coverage	0.28	0.02	-0.17	0.11	-0.01	0.13						
8 Phonics Coverage	0.35	0.37	0.14	0.11	0.38	0.23	0.12					
9 Basal Learning	0.34	0.09	-0.10	-0.01	0.09	0.26	0.89	0.20				
10 Phonics Learning	0.49	0.25	0.27	0.02	0.26	0.51	0.09	0.52	0.31			
11 First Grade Achievement	0.57	0.34	0.05	0.18	0.20	0.61	0.42	0.39	0.58	0.63		
12 Second Grade Achievement	0.45	0.39	-0.13	0.23	0.03	0.56	0.34	0.22	0.47	0.53	0.84	
Mean	63.0	2.2	74.6	0.6	15.5	52.9	293.8	52.3	270.3	30.2	1.7	1.6
Standard Deviation	6.7	1.0	3.9	0.5	8.2	10.8	63.5	12.5	68.4	9.4	1.2	1.2

Levels of significance: 0.05: r > 0.30; 0.01: r > 0.39.

APPENDIX J

Beta Coefficients Showing the Contribution of Children's Background Characteristics and Group Conditions to Successive Dependent Variables among High Aptitude Children (n = 44)

Independent Variables	Dependent Variables (Variable Numbers)						
	5	6	7	8	9	10	11[a]
1 Children's Aptitude	.18	.52*	.28	.22	-.02	.25*	.13
2 Children's SES	-.18	.07	-.08	.36*	.05	-.05	.14
3 Children's Age (months)	.32*	.25	-.15	.06	-.02	.19*	-.05
4 Children's Sex (m=0, f=1)	-.12	.21	.10	.12	-.15*	.03	.14
5 Group Size		.02	.01	.42*	.06	-.04	.12
6 Group Mean Aptitude			.01	-.07	.16	.17	.23
7 Basal Coverage				.06	.88**	-.66*	-.13
8 Phonics Coverage					.04	.33*	-.03
9 Basal Learning						.73*	.50
10 Phonics Learning							.27
R	.41	.63	.33	.62	.92	.75	.84
R^2 (percent)	16	40	11	38	85	57	70
Adjusted R^2 (percent)	8	32	3	27	81	46	61
$\sqrt{1 - R^2}$	.92	.77	.94	.79	.39	.66	.55

[a] Measure of standardized first greade reading achievement.

* Unstandardized coefficient is 2 to 4 times as large as the standard error.

** Unstandardized coefficient is 5 or more times as large as the standard error.

References

Alexander, K. L., Cook, M., and McDill, E. L. 1978. "Curriculum Tracking and Educational Stratification: Some Further Evidence." *American Sociological Review* 43:47–66.

Alexander, K. L. and Eckland, B. K. 1975a. "School Experience and Status Attainment." In *Adolescence and the Life Cycle,* ed. S. E. Dragastin and G. H. Elder, pp. 171–210. New York: Hemisphere.

———. 1975b. "Contextual Effects in the High School Attainment Process." *American Sociological Review* 40:402–416.

Alexander, K. L., Eckland, B. K., and Griffin, L. J. 1975. "The Wisconsin Model of Socioeconomic Achievement: A Replication." *American Journal of Sociology* 81:324–342.

Alexander, K. L. and McDill, E. L. 1976. "Selection and Allocation within Schools: Some Causes and Consequences of Curriculum Placement." *American Sociological Review* 41:963–980.

Alwin, D. F. and Otto, L. B. 1977. "High School Context Effects on Aspirations." *Sociology of Education* 50:259–273.

Anderson, R. C.; Reynolds, R. E.; Schallert, D. L.; and Goetz, E. T. 1977. "Frameworks for Comprehending Discourse." *American Educational Research Journal* 14:367–381.

Ariès, P. 1962. *Centuries of Childhood.* New York: Knopf.

Ausubel, D. P., Novak, J. D., and Hanesian, H. 1978. *Educational Psychology: A Cognitive View*. New York: Holt, Rinehart & Winston.

Averch, H. A.; Carroll, S. J.; Donaldson, T. S.; Kiesling, H. J.; and Pincus, J. 1972. *How Effective Is Schooling? A Critical Review and Synthesis of Research Findings*. Santa Monica, Calif.: Rand.

Barker Lunn, J. C. 1970. *Streaming in the Primary School*. London: National Foundation for Educational Research in England and Wales.

Baron, J. N. and Bielby, W. T. 1980. "Bringing the Firms Back In: Stratification, Segmentation, and the Organization of Work." *American Sociological Review* 45:737–765.

Barr, R. 1971. *Development of a Word Learning Task to Predict Success and Identify Methods by Which Kindergarten Children Learn to Read*. U.S. Office of Education, Final Report No. 9-E-125.

———. 1973–74. "Instructional Pace Differences and Their Effect on Reading Acquisition." *Reading Research Quarterly* 9:526–554.

———. 1975. "How Children Are Taught to Read: Grouping and Pacing." *School Review* 83:479–498.

———. 1983. "Content Coverage in Classrooms." In *International Encyclopedia of Education*, ed. T. Husen and T. N. Postlethwaite, n.p. Oxford: Pergamon.

Barr, R. and Dreeben, R. 1978. "Instruction in Classrooms." In *Review of Research in Education 5*, ed. L. S. Shulman, pp. 89–162. Itasca, Ill.: Peacock.

Bellack, A. A.; Kliebard, H. M.; Hyman, R. T.; and Smith, F. T. 1966. *The Language of the Classroom*. New York: Teachers College Press.

Bennett, N. 1976. *Teaching Styles and Pupil Progress*. London: Open Books.

Bennett, N. and Jordan, J. 1975. "A Typology of Teaching Styles in Primary Schools." *British Journal of Educational Psychology* 45:20–28.

Bidwell, C. E. 1965. "The School as a Formal Organization." In *Handbook of Organizations*, ed. J. G. March, pp. 972–1018. Chicago: Rand McNally.

Bidwell, C. E. and Kasarda, J. D. 1975. "School District Organization and Student Achievement." *American Sociological Review* 40:55–70.

———. 1980. "Conceptualizing and Measuring the Effects of School and Schooling." *American Journal of Education* 88:401–430.

Blau, P. M. and Duncan, O. D. 1967. *The American Occupational Structure*. New York: Wiley.

Bloom, B. S. 1968. "Learning for Mastery." *Evaluation Comment* (UCLA) 1:unpaginated.

———. 1976. *Human Characteristics and School Learning*. New York: McGraw-Hill.

Borg, W. R. 1965. "Ability Grouping in the Public Schools." *Journal of Experimental Education* 34:1–97.

Bowman, M. J. 1976. "Through Education to Earnings." *Proceedings of the National Academy of Education* 3:221–292.

Brookover, W.; Beady, C.; Flood, P.; Schweitzer, J.; and Wisenbaker, J. 1979. *School Social Systems and Student Achievement*. New York: Praeger.

Brophy, J. E. and Evertson, C. M. 1974. *Process-Product Correlations in the Texas Teacher Effectiveness Study*, University of Texas Research and Development Center for Teacher Education, Report No. 74-4. Austin, Tex.

Brown, B. W. and Saks, D. H. 1975. "The Production and Distribution of Cognitive Skills within Schools." *Journal of Political Economy* 83:571–593.

―――. 1980. "Production Technologies and Resource Allocations within Classrooms and Schools: Theory and Measurement." In *The Analysis of Educational Productivity: Issues in Microanalysis*, vol. 1, ed. R. Dreeben and J. A. Thomas, pp. 53–117. Cambridge: Ballinger.

Burkhead, J., Fox, T. G., and Holland, J. W. 1967. *Input and Output in Large-City High Schools*. Syracuse: Syracuse University Press.

Burr, M. Y. 1931. *A Study of Homogeneous Grouping*. New York: Teachers College Bureau of Publications.

Burstein, L. 1980. "The Role of Levels of Analysis in the Specification of Educational Effects." In *The Analysis of Educational Productivity: Issues in Microanalysis*, vol. 1, ed. R. Dreeben and J. A. Thomas, pp. 119–190. Cambridge: Ballinger.

Carroll, J. B. 1963. "A Model of School Learning." *Teachers College Record* 64:723–733.

Cohen, E. G.; Deal, T. D.; Meyer, J. W.; and Scott, R. W. 1976. *Organization and Instruction in Elementary Schools*. Stanford Center for Research and Development in Teaching, Technical Report No. 50. Stanford, Calif.

Coleman, J. S.; Campbell, E. Q.; Hobson, C. J.; McPartland, J.; Mood, A. J.; Weinfeld, F. D.; and York, R. L. 1966. *Equality of Educational Opportunity*. Washington: U.S. Government Printing Office.

Cronbach, L. J. 1975. "Beyond the Two Disciplines of Scientific Psychology." *American Psychologist* 30:116–127.

Cronbach, L. J. and Snow, R. E. 1977. *Aptitudes and Instructional Methods*. New York: Irvington.

Dahlöff, U. 1971. *Ability Grouping, Content Validity, and Curriculum Process Analysis*. New York: Teachers College Press.

Daniels, J. C. 1961. "The Effects of Streaming in the Primary School, II: A Comparison of Streamed and Unstreamed Schools." *British Journal of Educational Psychology* 31:119–127.

Doyle, W. 1978. "Paradigms for Research on Teacher Effectiveness." In *Review of Research in Education 5*, ed. L. S. Shulman, pp. 163–198. Itasca, Ill.: Peacock.

Dunkin, M. J. and Biddle, B. J. 1974. *The Study of Teaching*. New York: Holt, Rinehart & Winston.

Fägerlind, I. 1975. *Formal Education and Adult Earnings*. Stockholm: Almqvist & Wiksell.

Findley, W. G. and Bryan, M. M. 1970. *Ability Grouping, 1970: Status, Impact, and Alternatives*. Center for Educational Improvement. Athens, Ga.

Fisher, C. W.; Filby, N. N.; Marliave, R.; Cahen, L. S.; Dishaw, M. M.; Moore, J. E.; and Berliner, D. C. 1978. *Teaching Behaviors, Academic Learning Time and Student Achievement*. Final Report of Phase III-B, Beginning Teacher Evaluation Study. Technical Report V-1. Far West Laboratory for Educational Research and Development. San Francisco.

Flanders, N. A. 1965. *Teacher Influence, Pupil Attitudes, and Achievement*. U.S. Department of Health, Education, and Welfare Cooperative Research Monograph No. 12. Washington.

Gage, N. L. 1964. "Theories of Teaching." In *Theories of Learning and Instruction*, ed. E. R. Hilgard, pp. 268–285. Chicago: National Society for the Study of Education.

———. 1972. *Teacher Effectiveness and Teacher Education*. Palo Alto, Calif.: Pacific.

———. 1978. *The Scientific Basis of the Art of Teaching*. New York: Teachers College Press.

Gates, A. I. and MacGinitie, W. H. 1965. *Gates-MacGinitie Reading Tests*. New York: Teachers College Press.

Gates, A. I. and Russell, D. H. 1938. "Types of Materials, Vocabulary Burden, Word Analysis, and Other Factors in Beginning Reading, Part II." *Elementary School Journal* 39:119–128.

Glaser, R., ed. 1978. *Advances in Instructional Psychology*, vol. 1. Hillsdale, N.J.: Erlbaum.

Glass, G. V and Smith, M. L. 1978. *Meta-Analysis of Research on the Relationship of Class Size and Achievement*. San Francisco: Far West Laboratory for Educational Research and Development.

Goldberg, M. L., Passow, A. H., and Justman, J. 1966. *The Effects of Ability Grouping*. New York: Teachers College Press.

Good, T., Grouws, D., and Beckerman, T. 1978. "Curriculum Pacing: Some Empirical Data in Mathematics." *Journal of Curriculum Studies* 10:75–82.

Graham, P. A. 1980. "Whither Equality of Educational Opportunity." *Daedalus* 109:115–132.

Green, T. F. 1980. *Predicting the Behavior of the Educational System*. Syracuse: Syracuse University Press.

Greeno, J. G. 1978. "A Study of Problem Solving." In *Advances in Instructional Psychology*, vol. 1, ed. R. Glaser, pp. 13–75. Hillsdale, N.J.: Erlbaum.

Haller, A. O. and Portes, A. 1973. "Status Attainment Processes." *Sociology of Education* 46:51–91.

Hallinan, M. and Sørenson, A. B. 1981. "The Formation and Stability of Instructional Groups." Paper presented at the Annual Meeting of the American Sociological Association, Toronto, Canada.

Harnischfeger, A. and Wiley, D. E. 1976. "The Teaching-Learning Process in Elementary Schools: A Synoptic View." *Curriculum Inquiry* 6:5–43.

———. 1978. "Conceptual Issues in Models of School Learning." *Journal of Curriculum Studies* 3:215–231.

Hartill, R. M. 1936. *Homogeneous Grouping.* New York: Teachers College Bureau of Publications.

Hauser, R. M. 1969. "Schools and the Stratification Process." *American Journal of Sociology* 74:587–611.

———. 1970. "Context and Consex: A Cautionary Tale." *American Journal of Sociology* 75:645–664.

Heyns, B. 1974. "Social Selection and Stratification within Schools." *American Journal of Sociology* 79:1434–1451.

———. 1978. *Summer Learning and the Effects of Schooling.* New York: Academic.

Jencks, C. S. 1972. "The Coleman Report and the Conventional Wisdom." In *On Equality of Educational Opportunity,* ed. F. Mosteller and D. P. Moynihan, pp. 69–115. New York: Random House.

Jencks, C.; Smith, M.; Acland, H.; Bane, M. J.; Cohen, D.; Gintis, H.; Heyns, B.; and Michelson, S. 1972. *Inequality.* New York: Basic Books.

Kahl, J. A. 1953. "Educational and Occupational Aspirations of 'Common Man' Boys." *Harvard Educational Review* 23:186–203.

Karweit, N. 1976. "A Reanalysis of the Effect of Quantity of Schooling on Achievement." *Sociology of Education* 49:236–246.

Katzman, M. T. 1971. *The Political Economy of Urban Schools.* Cambridge: Harvard.

Kett, J. F. 1977. *Rites of Passage.* New York: Basic Books.

Kintsch, W. 1974. *The Representation of Meaning in Memory.* Hillsdale, N.J.: Erlbaum.

Lau, L. J. 1979. "Educational Production Functions." In *Economic Dimensions of Education,* ed. D. M. Windham, pp. 33–69. Washington: National Academy of Education.

Lesgold, A. M. and Curtis, M. E. 1981. "Learning to Read Words Efficiently." In *Interactive Processes in Reading,* ed. A. M. Lesgold and C. A. Perfetti, pp. 329–360. Hillsdale, N.J.: Erlbaum.

Lewin, K., Lippitt, R., and White, R. K. 1939. "Patterns of Aggressive Behavior in Experimentally Created Social Climates." *Journal of Social Psychology* 1:271–279.

Lipset, S. M., Trow, M. A., and Coleman, J. S. 1956. *Union Democracy.* Glencoe, Ill.: Free Press.

Lundgren, U. P. 1972. *Frame Factors and the Teaching Process.* Stockholm: Almqvist & Wiksell.

McDill, E. L. and Rigsby, L. C. 1973. *Structure and Process in Secondary Schools: The Academic Impact of Educational Climates.* Baltimore: Johns Hopkins University Press.

Medley, D. M. and Mitzel, H. E. 1958. "A Technique for Measuring Classroom Behavior." *Journal of Educational Psychology* 49:86–92.

Meux, M. and Smith, B. O. 1964. "Logical Dimensions of Teaching Behavior." In *Contemporary Research on Teacher Effectiveness,* ed. B. J. Biddle and W. J. Elena, pp. 127–164. New York: Holt, Rinehart & Winston.

Meyer, J. W. 1970. "The Charter: Conditions of Diffuse Socialization in Schools." In *Social Processes and Social Structures,* ed. W. R. Scott, pp. 564–578. New York: Holt, Rinehart & Winston.

———. 1977. "Education as an Institution." *American Journal of Sociology* 83:55–77.

———. 1980. "Levels of Educational Systems and Schooling Effects." In *The Analysis of Educational Productivity: Issues in Microanalysis,* vol. 2, ed. C. E. Bidwell and D. M. Windham, pp. 15–63. Cambridge: Ballinger.

Murnane, R. J. 1975. *The Impact of School Resources on the Learning of Inner City Children.* Cambridge: Ballinger.

Parsons, T. 1959. "The School Class as a Social System." *Harvard Educational Review* 29:297–318.

———. 1963. "Some Ingredients of a General Theory of Formal Organization." In *Structure and Process in Modern Societies,* ed. T. Parsons, pp. 59–96. Glencoe, Ill.: Free Press.

Resnick, L. B. 1976. "Task Analysis in Instructional Design: Some Cases from Mathematics." In *Cognition and Instruction,* ed. D. Klahr, pp. 51–80. Hillsdale, N.J.: Erlbaum.

Rist, R. C. 1970. "Student Social Class and Teacher Expectations: The Self-fulfilling Prophesy in Ghetto Education." *Harvard Educational Review* 40:411–451.

Rosenbaum, J. E. 1976. *Making Inequality.* New York: Wiley.

Rosenshine, B. 1971. *Teaching Behaviours and Student Achievement.* London: National Foundation for Educational Research in England and Wales.

———. 1979. "Content, Time, and Direct Instruction." In *Research on Teaching: Concepts, Findings, and Implications,* ed. P. Peterson and H. Walberg, pp. 28–56. Berkeley: McCutchan.

Rothkopf, E. Z. 1970. "The Concept of Mathemagenic Activities." *Review of Educational Research* 40:325–336.

Rutter, M.; Maughan, B.; Mortimore, P.; Ouston, J.; with Smith, A. 1979. *Fifteen Thousand Hours.* Cambridge: Harvard.

Scott, W. R. 1975. "Organizational Structure." In *Annual Review of Sociology I,* ed. A. Inkeles, J. S. Coleman, and N. Smelser, pp. 1–20. Palo Alto, Calif.: Annual Reviews.

Sewell, W. H., Haller, A. O., and Strauss, M. A. 1957. "Social Status and Educational and Occupational Aspiration." *American Sociological Review* 22:67–73.

Sewell, W. H. and Hauser, R. M. 1975. *Education, Occupation, and Earnings: Achievement in American Society.* New York: Academic.

Sewell, W. H., Hauser, R. M., and Featherman, D. L., eds. 1976. *Schooling and Achievement in American Society.* New York: Academic.

Sibley, E. 1942. "Some Demographic Clues to Stratification." *American Sociological Review* 7:322–330.

Simmel, G. 1950. *The Sociology of Georg Simmel.* Glencoe, Ill.: Free Press.

Smith, N. B. 1965. *American Reading Instruction.* Newark, Del.: International Reading Association.

Sørensen, A. B. and Hallinan, M. T. 1977. "A Reconceptualization of School Effects." *Sociology of Education* 50:273–289.

Stallings, J. 1975. "Implementation and Child Effects of Teaching Practices in Follow Through Classrooms." *Monographs of the Society for Research in Child Development,* Serial No. 163, Nos. 7–8.

Stephens, J. M. 1967. *The Process of Schooling.* New York: Holt, Rinehart & Winston.

Stouffer, S. A. 1962. "The Study of Mobility: Some Strategic Considerations." In *Social Research to Test Ideas,* ed. S. A. Stouffer, pp. 225–231. Glencoe, Ill.: Free Press.

Summers, A. A. 1979. *What Helps Fourth Grade Students to Read? A Pupil-, Classroom-, Program-Specific Investigation.* Research Paper No. 40. Philadelphia: Federal Reserve Bank of Philadelphia.

Summers, A. A. and Wolfe, B. L. 1974. *Equality of Educational Opportunity Quantified: A Production Function Approach.* Philadelphia: Federal Reserve Bank of Philadelphia.

———. 1977. "Do Schools Make a Difference?" *American Economic Review* 67:639–652.

Suppes, P. and Morningstar, M. 1972. *Computer Assisted Instruction at Stanford, 1966–68: Data, Models, and Evaluation of the Arithmetic Programs.* New York: Academic.

Taubman, P. and Wales, T. 1974. *Higher Education and Earnings: College as a Screening Device.* New York: McGraw-Hill.

Thomas, J. A. 1977. *Resource Allocation in Classrooms.* National Institute of Education, Final Report No. G-74-0037.

Walberg, H. J., ed. 1974. *Evaluating Educational Performance.* Berkeley: McCutchan.

———. 1977. "Psychology of Learning Environments: Behavioral, Structural, or Perceptual?" In *Review of Research in Education 4*, ed. L. S. Shulman, pp. 142–178. Itasca, Ill.: Peacock.

Weick, K. 1976. "Educational Organizations as Loosely Coupled Systems." *Administrative Science Quarterly* 21:1–19.

West, P. 1933. *A Study of Ability Grouping in the Elementary School.* New York: Teachers College Bureau of Publications.

Wiley, D. E. 1973. *Another Hour, Another Day: Quantity of Schooling, a Potent Path for Policy.* CEMREL Studies of Educative Processes, Report No. 3.

Wiley, D. E. and Harnischfeger, A. 1974. "Explosion of a Myth: Quantity of Schooling and Exposure to Instruction, Major Educational Vehicles." *Educational Researcher* 3:7–12.

Wilson, A. B. 1959. "Residential Segregation of Social Classes and Aspirations of High School Boys." *American Sociological Review* 24:836–845.

Index

187